Thomas Deville

The art of storytelling

Master the art of captivating storytelling

Avenet Edition

"Stories have become the default method of communicating information, so much so that we need to learn how to tell good stories so that our message can be heard."

Peter Guber

"What stays in someone's mind is a story. If you can tell a story, people will remember you and your message."

Andrew Stanton

"Stories are the vehicle by which we all transit into the future. They are the tools that enable us to cross the boundaries of human time and space."

Frank Rose

Contents

Introduction   **9**

Part 1: The foundations of storytelling   **13**

Chapter 1: The history of storytelling: from caves to
social media   15

Chapter 2: Why storytelling matters: the impact on
the human brain   43

Chapter 3: The key elements of a compelling story:
characters, plot and conflict   67

Chapter 4: The classic narrative structure: the
three-act rule   77

Part 2: Storytelling in marketing   **87**

Chapter 5: Brand storytelling: giving your company
a soul   89

Chapter 6: Examples of successful storytelling by
major brands   103

Chapter 7: Social media and storytelling: building a
community around your story   123

Part 3: Mastering the art of storytelling
133

Chapter 8: Finding the right story: brainstorming and ideation techniques   135

Chapter 9: The great storytelling masters: how to draw inspiration from their stories?   145

Chapter 10: Measuring the impact of your storytelling: performance indicators and return on investment   161

Chapter 11: Common storytelling mistakes and how to avoid them   169

Conclusion
179

Introduction

The power of stories is immense. They can move us, inspire us and transport us to new worlds. Stories can make us laugh, cry, think and act. They can connect people, transcend cultures and generations, and shape our understanding of ourselves and the world around us.

In "The Art of Storytelling", I invite you to explore this fascinating universe and discover how stories can be used effectively and creatively in marketing and communication. Whether you're an entrepreneur, marketer, author or simply a storytelling enthusiast, this book will guide you through the essential steps to mastering the art of storytelling and creating powerful, unforgettable stories.

Over the course of these pages, you'll discover how storytelling has evolved over time, and how it has become an essential tool for reaching and captivating your audience. Together we'll see why storytelling is so important and how it acts on our brains, forging lasting memories and deep emotions.

This book will also offer you practical tips and techniques for crafting captivating stories that resonate with your audience. You'll learn how to build authentic, engaging characters, structure your stories effectively and infuse emotion and humor into your stories. We'll also cover the importance of understanding and responding to the needs of your target audience to create stories that touch and inspire them.

In the world of marketing and communications, storytelling is an invaluable tool for creating lasting connections with your audience and giving your company a soul. By mastering the art of storytelling, you'll be able to stand out from the competition, arouse your customers' interest and curiosity, and inspire them to take action.

"The Art of Storytelling" is an invitation to plunge into the heart of this exciting universe and discover the secrets and techniques for telling stories that captivate, move and inspire. So get ready to embark on an extraordinary journey through the intricacies of storytelling, and let us guide you through the lessons and tips that will lead you to success in the art of unforgettable storytelling.

Now open this book, and let the adventure begin!

Your opinion counts!

*Once you've finished this book,
share your review on Amazon.*

*Your feedback will be useful for
future readers.*

*I look forward to seeing how this
book has impacted you.*

*Thank you in advance for your
contribution, and happy reading!*

Part 1: The foundations of storytelling

Chapter 1:

The history of storytelling: from caves to social media

This chapter traces the evolution of storytelling throughout history, showing how human beings have always been fascinated by narratives and how different forms of communication have shaped the way we tell stories.

1. The first stories: rock art and founding myths

Prehistoric visual communication

Let me tell you a story that goes back millennia, long before smartphones and social media invaded our lives. Imagine a time when men lived in caves, hunting mammoths to survive and lighting themselves with torches to ward off the darkness.

It was in this context that rock art was born, a form of prehistoric visual communication that bears witness to humanity's first attempts to tell stories and share experiences. Paintings and engravings on cave walls were a way for our ancestors to represent their daily lives, their dreams and their fears. Animals, hunting scenes and mysterious symbols were depicted with a charming simplicity.

One day, while on vacation in France, I had the opportunity to visit the famous Lascaux cave. I can tell you that I was dazzled by the beauty and complexity of the paintings that adorn its walls. It was as if our ancestors had wanted to convey a message to us through the ages, using a universal language: art.

Founding myths, on the other hand, are the earliest stories that have spanned generations and shaped people's beliefs. These epic tales featured gods, heroes and mythical creatures, and served to explain the mysteries of the universe and transmit cultural values. Greek myths, for example, have bequeathed us unforgettable characters such as Hercules, Perseus and Medusa.

These primitive forms of storytelling testify to mankind's innate thirst for telling and hearing stories. From prehistoric caves to today's social media, our need to share our experiences and give meaning to our existence has never wavered. And that, my friends, is why storytelling is so deeply rooted in our DNA.

Mythological stories and their role in ancient societies

Immerse yourself in a world of gods, goddesses, heroes and monsters. Myths played a crucial role in ancient societies, and their influence is still felt today.

Mythological tales were much more than mere entertainment; they reflected the beliefs, values and aspirations of the peoples who created them. By exploring the complex relationships between gods and humans, these stories gave meaning to an often incomprehensible and unpredictable world. They also served to legitimize the social order and teach moral lessons.

One day, at a conference, I met a professor who told me a fascinating anecdote. He explained how Greek myths, for example, were used to justify the supremacy of the gods over man and the importance of respecting divine laws. The story of Prometheus, who stole fire from the gods to give it to man, is an excellent example. For transgressing the divine order, Prometheus was condemned to be chained to a rock and suffer eternal punishment. This story warns of the dangers of hubris and disobedience to divine laws.

Myths were also vectors of social cohesion, reinforcing a sense of belonging to a community.

Mythological tales were often told at ceremonies and religious festivals, uniting people around shared values and beliefs. The Homeric epics, the Iliad and the Odyssey, were recited at banquets and competitions, celebrating the heroes' exploits and reminding listeners of the virtues they were expected to embody.

Finally, myths have also served as a source of inspiration for artists, writers and philosophers. Mythological tales have been adapted and reinvented over the centuries, providing inexhaustible material for artistic and literary creation. Tragic love stories, like that of Orpheus and Eurydice, have been immortalized in poetry, painting and music, echoing our own emotions and experiences.

They have shaped ancient societies, giving meaning to the world, strengthening community ties and inspiring art and literature. Their impact on our cultural heritage is undeniable, and they continue to nourish our imagination and our quest for meaning down the ages.

2. The development of writing: from clay tablets to parchment

The evolution of writing systems

The evolution of writing systems is a fascinating story that goes back thousands of years, and shows just how ingenious human beings are when it comes to conveying ideas and stories.

The journey begins with the first forms of writing, pictograms, which appeared around 3,200 B.C. These early writing systems used symbols to represent objects or concepts. Imagine drawing a sun to represent the day, or a moon to represent the night. It was a rudimentary way of communicating, but it was a start.

Then, around 3,000 BC, the Sumerians developed the cuneiform writing system. Engraved on clay tablets using a pointed reed, these writings were made up of wedge-shaped signs, hence the name "cuneiform". Cuneiform made it possible to record not only stories, but also laws, contracts and lists of goods. It was a major breakthrough in the history of writing and storytelling.

Let's move on to ancient Egypt, where hieroglyphics were used to tell stories and record history. Hieroglyphics were a complex writing system, consisting of over 700 signs representing objects, ideas and sounds. They were engraved on walls, monuments and papyrus, and were deciphered thanks to the famous Rosetta Stone, discovered in 1799.

Over the centuries, writing systems have developed and diversified. The Phoenicians created a linear alphabet, which was later adapted by the Greeks and Romans. The Latin alphabet, used to write many modern languages, including French and English, is a direct legacy of this evolution.

The invention of parchment and paper also played a crucial role in the dissemination of stories and ideas. Parchment, made from animal skins, was more resistant and durable than clay tablets and papyrus. As for paper, invented in China in the 2nd century BC, it revolutionized the way stories were written and shared, making writing more accessible and transportable.

Why am I telling you all this, you ask? The evolution of writing systems has been an essential driving force in the history of storytelling. From pictograms to cuneiform, hieroglyphics to the Latin alphabet, each step has enabled human beings to communicate better and share their stories, ideas and knowledge, laying the foundations for our rich literary and cultural heritage.

Passing on stories through the generations

Passing stories down through the generations is an essential aspect of storytelling and the preservation of our cultural heritage. Stories have been passed down from generation to generation in many different ways, since the dawn of time.

Before the invention of writing, the transmission of stories relied mainly on oral tradition. Storytellers were respected members of society, using their memory and talent to tell epic tales, legends and myths. These stories were often told at ceremonies, feasts or around campfires, and served to teach life lessons, explain the mysteries of the universe, entertain and strengthen social bonds within the community.

The advent of writing radically changed the way stories were passed on. Clay tablets, parchment and papyrus made it possible to record stories for future generations, preserving history and knowledge. It also enabled stories to be disseminated across geographical and cultural boundaries, broadening audiences and creating an exchange of ideas and traditions between different civilizations.

Over time, the invention of the printing press and the democratization of access to books facilitated the transmission of stories to an even wider audience. Stories could thus be disseminated more rapidly and more widely, reaching people from all walks of life. Libraries, both public and private, have become conservatories of our literary and cultural heritage, enabling future generations to discover and appreciate the stories of the past.

Today, social media and digital technologies play an increasingly important role in storytelling. Blogs, podcasts, online videos and content-sharing platforms offer new opportunities for telling and sharing stories, enabling everyone to be both storyteller and spectator. These modern tools have also contributed to the reinvention of oral tradition, with live performances, poetry slams and digital storytelling sessions.

The transmission of stories across generations is a process that has evolved over time, adapting to technological and cultural innovations. Whether it's storytellers around a campfire or videos shared on social networks, the essence of storytelling remains the same: telling stories that captivate, move and inspire, helping to preserve our cultural heritage and strengthen our common humanity.

3. Storytellers and troubadours: the oral tradition

The art of public storytelling

The art of public storytelling is an age-old tradition that dates back to the days when human societies were primarily based on oral communication. Storytellers and troubadours were key figures in the transmission of a community's history, culture and values.

Storytellers were masters of the art of oratory, able to captivate their audience's attention thanks to their charisma, expressiveness and talent for structuring and animating narratives. They often used memorization techniques, such as repetitive formulas, rhymes and refrains, to help retain story details and facilitate their transmission.

Troubadours were medieval itinerant performers who sang and told stories of courtly love, adventure and bravery, usually accompanied by a musical instrument. They were highly prized for their ability to entertain and move audiences, adapting their repertoire to suit the tastes and concerns of their audience.

Here are some key elements of public storytelling:

1. **Connecting with the audience**: Storytellers and troubadours sought to establish an emotional bond with their audience, making eye contact, modulating their voice and using expressive gestures to reinforce the message of their story.

2. **Build a captivating plot**: The stories told had to be captivating enough to hold the audience's attention. Storytellers used narrative techniques such as suspense, plot twists and engaging characters to create a tale that captivated the audience from beginning to end.

3. **Using humor and emotion**: Storytellers and troubadours used humor and emotion to engage their audiences, alternating comic and dramatic moments to maintain interest and elicit an emotional response.

4. **Personalize the story**: Storytellers and troubadours knew how to adapt their tale to suit their audience, incorporating local elements, familiar characters or personal anecdotes to make the story more relevant and appealing.

5. **Memorization and improvisation**: Storytellers and troubadours had to master

the art of memorization to retain the details of their stories, while at the same time being able to improvise and adapt to their audience's reactions.

The art of public storytelling is a precious legacy from our past, which continues to inspire and influence today's storytellers. The techniques and principles that have guided storytellers and troubadours through the centuries remain relevant and effective in touching the hearts and minds of our audiences.

Folk legends and fables

Folk legends and fables are stories that have been passed down from generation to generation, mainly through oral tradition. These tales have an educational, moral and entertaining function, and are deeply rooted in the imagination and culture of the peoples who created them.

- **Legends**: Legends are tales that often blend historical facts with fantastical elements to create epic, captivating stories. They feature heroes and heroines, gods and monsters, adventures and quests, betrayals and forbidden loves. Legends often have a historical or geographical basis, but they are also influenced by mythology, religion and popular beliefs. Among the best-known legends are King Arthur and the Knights of the Round Table, Robin Hood and the myth of Tristan and Isolde.

- **Fables**: Fables are short, didactic stories that use animals, objects or supernatural beings to illustrate moral lessons and universal truths. These stories are often built around a conflict situation or dilemma, and usually conclude with an explicit or implicit moral that teaches readers a lesson about life and human relationships. The most famous fables are undoubtedly those of Aesop, an ancient Greek storyteller whose stories have been adapted and reinterpreted in many cultures and eras, such as La Fontaine's fables in France.

Folk legends and fables have played an essential role in preserving and transmitting the collective wisdom, values and beliefs of peoples across time and space. Storytellers and troubadours were the guardians of this cultural memory, and their talent for captivating storytelling enabled these tales to survive and continue to inspire and instruct future generations.

Even today, folk legends and fables remain inexhaustible sources of inspiration for storytellers, writers and artists, who draw on these treasures of imagination and wisdom to create new stories and new forms of artistic expression. The teachings and emotions conveyed by these universal tales continue to resonate in our hearts and minds, reminding us that, whatever our origins and differences, we all share the same humanity and fundamental aspirations.

4. Printing and the book revolution

Gutenberg's impact on storytelling

Johannes Gutenberg's invention of the printing press in the mid-15th century was a veritable revolution in the history of storytelling and communication in general. Before that time, stories and knowledge were transmitted mainly by oral tradition and handwritten copy, which greatly limited their dissemination and accessibility. With the creation of the printing press and the use of movable metal type, Gutenberg changed all that and ushered in a new age of information.

The democratization of stories

The printing press made it possible to produce books in large quantities and at much lower cost, making stories and knowledge accessible to a much wider audience than before. This democratized the dissemination of stories, and enabled people from all walks of life to enrich themselves through reading and the exchange of ideas. This helped spread culture and education throughout Europe and the world.

The rise of authors and publishers

Thanks to the printing press, new professions and new opportunities emerged. Authors were able to disseminate their works to a wider audience, and publishers emerged as intermediaries between authors and readers, playing a crucial role in the selection, promotion and distribution of stories. This also encouraged the creation of new literary and artistic forms, which have continued to enrich humanity's cultural and creative heritage.

Language and text standardization

Printing helped standardize languages and texts, setting orthographic and grammatical standards and contributing to the emergence of national languages and literary canons. This strengthened peoples' sense of belonging and cultural identity, while paving the way for the translation and dissemination of stories and ideas across linguistic and cultural boundaries.

The circulation of ideas and the emergence of critical thinking

Finally, printing played a decisive role in the circulation of ideas and the emergence of critical thinking, facilitating debate and the confrontation of opinions, and promoting the dissemination of scientific, philosophical and artistic knowledge. The great intellectual and cultural movements of the modern era, such as the Renaissance, the Reformation and the Enlightenment, owe much to Gutenberg's invention and the rise of printing.

Gutenberg's impact on the dissemination of stories was immense, and marked a decisive turning point in the history of communication and culture. The printing press made stories and knowledge accessible to a much wider public, fostered the creation and dissemination of ideas, and helped shape our world's cultural identity and diversity.

The first bestsellers and the development of literary genres

With the advent of the printing press, the literary world experienced an unprecedented boom. Stories began to circulate more widely, and readers developed an insatiable appetite for captivating tales. This led to the appearance of the first bestsellers and the development of specific literary genres to cater for the public's diverse interests and tastes.

The first bestsellers

Among the first bestsellers was the Gutenberg Bible, printed in 1455. Not only was this the first edition of the Bible to be printed, but it was also the starting point for a veritable craze for printed books. Other important works, such as Diderot and d'Alembert's Encyclopédie and the works of Shakespeare, also enjoyed great commercial success, helping to establish the reputations of their authors and shape the literary tastes of the time.

The novel

With the development of the printing press and the democratization of reading, the novel emerged as a major literary genre, offering readers long, complex stories that explore human nature, social relationships and moral dilemmas. Over the centuries, the novel has evolved to encompass numerous sub-genres, such as the realistic novel, the Gothic novel, the detective story, the romance novel and science fiction, to name but a few.

Poetry

Poetry also enjoyed a remarkable boom in the age of printing, with poets such as William Shakespeare, John Donne and John Milton making literary history with their verse. Poems were often published in collections, enabling authors to reach a wide audience and express their emotions, ideas and observations about the world around them.

The theater

Thanks to the printing press, plays could be performed and read by a much wider audience than before. Playwrights such as Shakespeare, Molière and Racine gained international renown thanks to their printed works, which were performed on stages all over the world and influenced the development of modern theater.

Essays and pamphlets

The printing press also facilitated the dissemination of ideas through essays and pamphlets, which were widely used to promote political, religious and philosophical opinions. Authors such as Michel de Montaigne, Thomas Paine and Jonathan Swift used these formats to express their ideas, provoke debate and influence public opinion.

Ultimately, the printing press and the book revolution greatly contributed to the development of literary genres and the emergence of the first bestsellers. This evolution enabled authors to reach a wider audience and express themselves in a variety of formats and styles.

5. Cinema, radio and television: the mass media

Pioneers of visual and audio storytelling

Mass media such as film, radio and television have revolutionized the way stories are told and consumed, opening up new possibilities for presenting visual and aural narratives. Among the pioneers of visual and aural storytelling are directors, scriptwriters, producers and radio hosts who have left their mark on media history by creating innovative and influential works.

- **Cinema**: The early days of cinema were marked by pioneers such as the Lumière brothers, who made the first film to be shown in public, "La Sortie de l'usine Lumière à Lyon", in 1895. Other directors, such as Georges Méliès, were quick to understand the potential of cinema to tell fantastic and visually impressive stories, as witnessed by his 1902 film, "Le Voyage dans la Lune". Over time, cinema has become an artistic medium in its own right, with directors such as Alfred Hitchcock, Orson Welles, Akira Kurosawa and Stanley Kubrick pushing the boundaries of visual storytelling.

- **Radio**: Radio offered a means of sound communication that enabled stories to be broadcast to a massive audience, without the geographical and economic constraints of print media. Radio programs such as Orson Welles' "The War of the Worlds", broadcast in 1938, demonstrated the power of sound storytelling to captivate audiences and arouse strong emotions. Radio dramas, comedies and soap operas were created to entertain, inform and educate listeners through captivating storytelling.

- **Television**: Television has combined the strengths of film and radio to create a new mass medium capable of reaching an even wider audience. Pioneers of television storytelling, such as Paddy Chayefsky and Rod Serling, created groundbreaking shows like "Marty" and "The Twilight Zone", which demonstrated television's potential for telling complex, emotionally rich stories.

Since then, television has evolved to encompass a wide range of genres and formats, including drama series, sitcoms, documentaries and reality shows.

- **Technological innovations**: Technological advances have also played a crucial role in the evolution of visual and aural storytelling. Innovations such as Technicolor, Cinemascope and stereophonic sound have enabled filmmakers to create more immersive and impressive cinematic experiences. On television, advances in image resolution and display technology have made television storytelling richer and more detailed than ever.

These pioneers of visual and aural storytelling laid the foundations of modern mass media and demonstrated the power of stories to captivate, educate and inspire generations of listeners and viewers. Their innovations and creativity paved the way for countless other creators who continue to push the boundaries of storytelling and explore new ways of telling stories through film, radio and television. Thanks to their work, stories have been able to reach a wider and more diverse audience, making storytelling an essential part of modern culture.

Democratizing access to stories

The democratization of access to stories is another crucial aspect of the evolution of storytelling. Before the advent of mass media, stories were often reserved for an elite or restricted group of people. However, with the development of cinema, radio and television, stories began to reach a much wider audience, transcending geographical, cultural and socio-economic boundaries.

Radio played an essential role in democratizing access to stories as early as the 1920s. Radio broadcasts enabled families to gather around a receiver to listen to stories, plays and reports, broadcast live or recorded. Oral storytelling thus regained a central place in daily life, in households of all social classes.

Cinema has also contributed to the democratization of storytelling, offering captivating visual experiences and creating narrative universes that have touched the hearts and minds of audiences. Films, accessible to a wide range of viewers, have made it possible to tell complex and ambitious stories, both familiar and foreign, which have opened the door to understanding and empathy between different cultures.

As for television, it revolutionized the way stories were consumed by bringing them directly into the home. Viewers had access to a wide range of genres and narrative formats, from drama series to sitcoms, documentaries and reality shows. Television has also made it possible to follow stories over long periods, with characters and story arcs evolving over the seasons.

Finally, the digital age has given rise to new storytelling platforms, such as podcasts, video streaming platforms and social networks. These new media have further expanded access to stories, enabling independent creators to share their tales with the world, and offering consumers an almost limitless choice of content to discover.

The democratization of access to stories has thus transformed our relationship with narratives, and enabled an ever-increasing number of people to immerse themselves in captivating stories, to learn, to escape and to connect with each other in ways never seen before.

6. Digital and social media: the age of connectivity

Content-sharing platforms and virality

The digital age and social media! These platforms have transformed the way we consume and share stories, and even created opportunities for new forms of storytelling. Let me tell you how it's worked.

Content-sharing platforms such as YouTube, Instagram, TikTok and others have given rise to a new generation of content creators and storytellers. These platforms enable users to share their own stories in a variety of formats, such as videos, photos, text or podcasts. The ease of access and the ability to reach a global audience have enabled emerging talents to make a name for themselves and build communities around their stories.

Virality is a phenomenon closely linked to these platforms. The term refers to the speed with which content spreads and becomes popular on the Internet. The appeal of successful storytelling, particularly when combined with powerful visual or audio elements, can trigger a chain reaction, where millions of people share, comment on and react to a story. This virality makes it possible to reach massive audiences in record time, something unimaginable in the pre-digital era.

Social media have also changed the face of storytelling. Platforms like Twitter and Facebook enable users to share stories and connect with others with similar interests. These online interactions can give rise to in-depth discussions, lively debates and exchanges of ideas that enrich and expand the stories shared.

What's more, social media has enabled brands and companies to get closer to their audiences by sharing stories that humanize their image and reinforce their values. Thanks to these platforms, brands can engage in authentic conversations with their customers, gather testimonials and feedback, and create storytelling campaigns that evoke emotion and build audience loyalty.

The age of connectivity has radically transformed the storytelling landscape. Content-sharing platforms and social media have made storytelling more accessible, diverse and participatory than ever before. Through this increased connectivity, stories continue to evolve, adapt and reach an ever wider and more engaged audience.

The role of influencers and content creators in modern storytelling

In the modern world of storytelling, influencers and content creators play a crucial role.

These charismatic and talented individuals have leveraged digital platforms to build communities and share their stories with a wide audience. So what exactly do they do, and why are they so important to storytelling today? Let me explain.

1. **Brand ambassadors**: Influencers are often called upon by brands to promote their products or services, as they benefit from an engaged and loyal audience. As storytellers, influencers are able to weave narratives around these products that make them desirable and appealing to their audience. Their recommendations are often perceived as more authentic and credible than traditional advertising.

2. **Creating trends and buzz**: Content creators and influencers are often at the forefront of trends and can help create a buzz around certain stories or ideas. Their impact can be enormous, and their persuasive power can turn a story into a viral phenomenon.

3. **Expertise and education**: Some influencers and content creators specialize in specific fields, such as fashion, technology, health or education. Their expertise enables them to share informative and educational stories that help their subscribers acquire new skills or improve their understanding of a particular subject.

4. **Inspiration and motivation**: Content creators and influencers often share their own personal experiences, challenges and successes in order to inspire and motivate their audience. These authentic, heartfelt stories can create a deep emotional bond with subscribers and encourage them to pursue their own dreams and goals.

5. **Entertainment and engagement**: Content creators and influencers know how to capture their audience's attention with entertaining and engaging content. Their talent for entertaining and innovative storytelling helps build audience loyalty and keeps them coming back for more.

Influencers and content creators have become key players in the modern storytelling landscape.

Their ability to weave compelling narratives, set trends and inspire their audiences makes them invaluable to brands and companies seeking to establish an authentic and lasting connection with their customers. What's more, they enrich our daily experience by sharing stories that entertain, inform and inspire us.

Chapter 2:

Why storytelling is important: the impact on the human brain

This chapter explores why storytelling is so important to us, focusing on the different impacts it has on our brain and psychology. The aim is to show that stories are not only entertaining, but also play a crucial role in our cognitive and emotional development.

1. The importance of emotion: stories that touch the heart

The role of emotions in decision-making

Emotions play a vital role in our decision-making process. They influence our perception of situations, our reactions and our choices. So how do emotions play a part in decision-making, and why are they so important to storytelling? Let's delve into this fascinating question.

Emotions guide our attention

When we feel emotions, our brains focus on information relevant to those emotions. For example, if you're angry, you're more likely to notice elements that reinforce that anger. Emotional stories capture our attention and make us more attentive to the details and messages conveyed.

Emotions facilitate memorization

Emotionally charged events are generally easier to remember. Our brains tend to attach greater importance to emotional memories and retain them longer. Stories that evoke strong emotions are therefore more likely to remain etched in our memory.

Emotions influence our judgment

Our emotions have a significant impact on our perception and judgment. For example, if you feel sympathy for a character, you're more likely to excuse his or her mistakes or approve of his or her actions. Stories that touch our emotions can thus lead us to modify our point of view on a subject or identify with characters.

Emotions determine our actions

Emotions can motivate us to act or avoid certain situations. For example, fear can prompt us to flee from danger, while curiosity can drive us to explore new horizons. Stories that generate strong emotions are capable of inspiring audiences to take action, whether to buy a product, share an experience or support a cause.

Emotions strengthen social bonds

Emotions are contagious and have the power to create bonds between individuals. When we share emotions with others, we feel a deeper connection and mutual understanding. Emotional stories can strengthen bonds within a community or group.

Emotions are at the heart of our decision-making process, influencing our attention, memory, judgment, actions and social relationships. By appealing to the emotions, storytelling can touch the audience's heart, facilitate message transmission and create a lasting impact. Emotional stories are not only captivating, they can also inspire, motivate and bring us closer together.

How stories stimulate empathy and emotional connection

Stories have the power to stimulate empathy and create deep emotional connections between people. This is due to several psychological and neurological mechanisms that come into play when we listen to or read stories. Let's discover together how stories promote empathy and emotional connection.

- **Character identification**: When we follow a story, we often identify with the characters, especially the protagonist. We put ourselves in their shoes, feeling their emotions, desires and fears as if we were experiencing them ourselves. This identification enables us to better understand the motivations and emotions of others, fostering our empathy and emotional connection.

- **Mental simulation**: Stories allow us to have fictional experiences and explore situations we've never encountered in reality. Our brains simulate these experiences as if we were actually living them, activating the same brain areas as those involved in real-life experiences. This mental simulation helps us to develop empathy, enabling us to better understand and feel the emotions and situations of others.

- **Sharing emotions**: Stories make us feel a wide range of emotions, from joy and sadness to anger and fear. By sharing these emotions with others, we strengthen our emotional connection and mutual understanding. Stories can create strong bonds between people, even if they don't know each other personally.

- **Mirror neurons**: Mirror neurons are brain cells that activate both when we perform an action and when we observe someone else performing the same action. They play a crucial role in our ability to understand and feel the emotions of others. Stories, by depicting the actions and emotions of characters, stimulate these mirror neurons and thus foster our empathy and emotional connection.

- **Shared vulnerability**: Stories often invite us to explore difficult situations, conflicts and moments of vulnerability. By sharing these emotional experiences, we open up to others and create a space for connection and mutual support. In this way, stories can help us overcome our fears, prejudices and differences, strengthening our empathy and common humanity.

Stories have the unique power to stimulate empathy and create deep emotional connections between people. They enable us to put ourselves in other people's shoes, share emotions and experiences, and strengthen our mutual understanding. By mastering the art of storytelling, we can touch the hearts of our audience and create a lasting impact on their lives.

2. Memorization and engagement: stories that stick in the mind

The human brain and the preference for structured narratives

The human brain has an innate preference for structured narratives. This preference is rooted in our evolution and history as a species. Stories have helped us understand our environment, learn from our experiences and convey important knowledge and values. Let's take a look at how structured stories leave their mark on the mind and why our brains prefer them.

Narrative coherence

Our brains are constantly searching for patterns, connections and causal relationships to make sense of the world around us. Structured narratives provide a coherent, logical framework that facilitates this understanding. By following a sequence of events and relationships between characters, we can better grasp the causes and consequences of actions, facilitating memorization and engagement.

Selective attention

Well-structured stories capture our attention and help us focus on the most important and relevant elements. By eliminating distractions and superfluous information, stories allow us to immerse ourselves fully in the story and become emotionally involved. This selective attention facilitates memorization and the anchoring of information in our long-term memory.

Repetition and memorization

Structured narratives often use repetition techniques and familiar narrative patterns to reinforce key messages and facilitate memorization. By repeating important information and presenting it in different forms, our brains are more likely to retain it and integrate it into our long-term memory.

Mental images

Well-constructed stories enable us to visualize events, places and characters in our minds. These mental images are easier to remember than abstract or decontextualized information. By creating vivid, detailed mental images, structured narratives enhance our engagement and ability to retain information.

Emotional impact

Structured stories touch us at the very core of our being, provoking emotional responses. Emotions are closely linked to our memory and engagement, reinforcing memories and motivating us to act. By eliciting strong emotions and associating them with key messages, structured stories leave a lasting impression on the mind.

Our brains prefer structured narratives because of their ability to facilitate comprehension, memorization and engagement. Well-constructed stories exploit our natural tendency to look for patterns and causal relationships, while captivating our attention, reinforcing our memories and eliciting emotional responses. By mastering the art of structured storytelling, you'll be able to touch your targets' brains, and therefore touch their hearts first and foremost.

Story-based memorization techniques

It's interesting to note that the human brain tends to retain information more easily when it's presented in narrative form. One of the reasons for this is that stories help to make sense of information that is often complex or abstract.

Personally, I've noticed that when I want to remember important facts or key figures for a presentation, I often incorporate them into a story or anecdote to anchor them more easily in my memory. For example, to remember key dates in art history, I've created an imaginary story in which historical figures meet in different museums around the world, at key moments in art history.

Similarly, in the marketing field, brands have long understood the importance of storytelling in capturing the attention of their audiences and arousing their commitment. For example, the Nike brand has succeeded in building a genuine community of fans through advertising campaigns featuring inspiring stories about famous sportsmen and women.

As part of my research for this book, I discovered a story-based memorization method called the place method. This technique involves associating each item to be memorized with a specific place in a mental pathway. By imagining a story unfolding in this pathway, we can then more easily retain the information associated with each place. This method has been used since Antiquity, and is still taught today in some business and management schools. It is, however, rather difficult to master.

3. Mirror neurons and the emotional contagion effect

How the brain imitates characters' emotions and actions

Mirror neurons are neurons that activate both when we perform an action and when we observe someone else performing the same action. They play a crucial role in our ability to understand the intentions and emotions of others, and are particularly active when we are immersed in a captivating story.

For example, I've noticed that when I watch a horror movie, my emotions are synchronized with those of the characters on screen. If a character is terrified, I tend to feel the same, and if a character triumphs, I feel a renewed sense of hope. Similarly, if I read a book in which a character achieves something great, I often feel inspired to do something similar myself.

This shows just how much stories can influence our emotional state, and even cause us to act in a certain way. Brands that manage to captivate their audiences with compelling stories can therefore have a powerful impact on their behavior.

Mirror neurons have also been studied for their role in empathy and understanding the emotions of others. By watching or reading a story, mirror neurons can activate and allow us to feel the emotions of the characters, which can lead to greater empathy and understanding of others. For example, read a novel in which the main character has lost a loved one, and you may feel deep sadness and empathy for that character. This experience helps you to better understand the pain of those who have experienced such a loss in real life.

Using this knowledge of mirror neurons and the emotional contagion effect, marketers and communicators can create stories that elicit a specific emotional response from their audience. For example, an advert for a charity that shows the difficult conditions in which people in need live can evoke compassion in viewers and encourage them to make a donation.

Mirror neurons and the emotional contagion effect are important elements to consider when creating stories. By understanding how our brains react to stories and characters' emotions, we can create more effective and engaging stories.

Sharing experiences through storytelling

Sharing experiences through storytelling is a key element of the power of stories on our brain and behavior. When we listen to or read a story, our brain is activated in a way that creates a personal experience for us, even if we've never had that experience before. Our brain's mirror neurons are activated, enabling us to feel the emotions and sensations described in the story.

That's why stories can be so powerful in connecting people. When we share a personal experience through a story, we create an emotional bond with our audience. They can feel what we felt, and understand the feelings we experienced. This can be particularly useful for brands and companies looking to establish an emotional connection with their audience.

Let's take the example of a company that manufactures sports shoes. Rather than simply touting the features of their product, they could tell the story of an athlete who overcame obstacles to achieve his or her goal, including using their famous shoes. By telling this story, the company creates an emotional bond with the public, who can recognize themselves in the challenges and obstacles overcome by the athlete. The public may also associate the company with this inspiring story, and be more inclined to buy its products.

Stories can also be useful for teaching and imparting knowledge. By telling stories about concrete situations, teachers can help students better understand and retain abstract concepts. Stories are also an effective way of teaching moral lessons and values. Fables, for example, have been used for centuries to teach children life lessons.

Finally, stories can help give meaning to our lives and experiences. By telling our own story, we can reflect on our own lives and find meaning and understanding in the events we have experienced. Stories can also help us imagine a different future and work towards personal or professional goals.

Sharing experiences through storytelling is a key part of the impact of stories on our brains and behavior. Stories can make emotional connections with audiences, teach lessons and values, and help make sense of our lives and experience. That's why storytelling has become an essential part of effective communication and persuasion in everything from advertising and education to politics and social media.

4. Persuasion and influence: stories that change minds

The psychological mechanisms of narrative persuasion

Narrative persuasion is a process by which stories can influence people's thoughts, attitudes and behaviors. It is a form of persuasion that uses stories rather than logical arguments to convince the audience. Stories have been used to persuade people for thousands of years, but scientific research has recently begun to explain the psychological mechanisms underlying this persuasion.

One of the key mechanisms of narrative persuasion is identification. When people identify with a character in a story, they are more likely to adopt that character's beliefs and attitudes. For example, if a story tells of a character who has overcome a difficult challenge, listeners may identify with that character and be more inclined to believe that challenges can be overcome.

Another important mechanism is emotion. Stories that evoke intense emotions are more likely to influence people's attitudes and behaviors than stories that do not. Emotions can act as a signal of the story's relevance to the listener, and can also reinforce the story's impact by activating brain centers linked to memory and learning.

Narrative persuasion can also be facilitated by the use of metaphors and analogies. These tools can help listeners understand abstract concepts by relating them to concrete, familiar experiences. Metaphors can also help elicit emotions and reinforce identification by evoking images and emotional associations.

By understanding these psychological mechanisms, storytellers and marketing professionals can create more effective stories that are more likely to influence listeners' attitudes and behaviors. However, it's important to stress that narrative persuasion isn't always positive. Stories can be used to manipulate people into believing things that aren't true. It is therefore essential that storytellers and marketing professionals use this power responsibly and ethically.

Narrative persuasion is an effective method of influencing people's attitudes and behaviors. The psychological mechanisms of identification, emotion and metaphor can all be used to create stories that are more likely to have an impact on the audience. However, it's important that storytellers and marketing professionals use this method responsibly and ethically.

The role of storytelling in advertising and propaganda

Storytelling plays a crucial role in advertising and propaganda. Advertisers and propagandists often use stories to influence people's attitudes and behavior towards a product, a person or an ideology.

- **Advertising** uses storytelling to sell products or services by creating stories that evoke emotions in consumers. For example, Apple's "Think Different" advertising campaign created a story that celebrated people who have changed the world, and associated this image with the Apple brand. Similarly, Nike's "Just Do It" ad campaign tells an inspiring story of self-transcendence and achievement, while associating the brand with this image.

- **Propaganda** also uses storytelling to manipulate public opinion in favor of an ideology or political regime. Propagandists create stories that arouse strong emotions to influence people's attitudes towards a cause or an enemy. For example, Nazi propaganda used stories to demonize Jews and other enemies of the regime, creating a sense of unity and support for the regime.

However, it's important to note that the use of storytelling in advertising and propaganda can be manipulative and misleading. The stories used can be exaggerated or even completely false, creating a biased or erroneous image of a product, person or ideology.

So it's essential to understand that storytelling can be a powerful tool for influencing attitudes and behaviors, but again, it's important to use it ethically and responsibly.

Overall, storytelling is a persuasive technique that can be used for both positive and negative purposes. Advertisers and propagandists use it to influence people's attitudes and behavior towards products, people or ideologies. However, it is important to consider the ethics and veracity of the stories used, as their influence can be considerable.

5. The pleasure of listening: captivating stories

The brain mechanisms responsible for story engagement

Stories have the ability to captivate our attention and immerse us in a world different from our own. This is due to a series of brain mechanisms that are activated when we listen to or read a story.

1. First, there's the activation of the area of the brain called the prefrontal cortex, which is responsible for planning, organization and analysis. When we listen to a story, this area is activated as our brains try to understand the narrative structure and link the various events together.

2. Then there's the activation of the amygdala, which is responsible for regulating emotions. When we listen to a story, we can feel a range of emotions, from joy and sadness to fear and excitement. The amygdala is therefore activated to regulate these emotions and enable us to connect emotionally to the story.

3. In addition, there is activation of Broca's area, which is responsible for language production. This area is activated when we listen to a story, as our brain tries to understand the words and phrases that are used, and relate them to the mental images we have of the story.

4. Finally, there's the activation of Wernicke's area, which is responsible for language comprehension. This area is activated when we listen to a story, as our brains try to understand the meaning of the words and phrases used, and relate them to the mental images we have of the story.

Stories have the ability to capture our attention and immerse us in a world different from our own, by activating a series of brain mechanisms such as the prefrontal cortex, amygdala, Broca's area and Wernicke's area. By understanding these mechanisms, content creators can design more engaging and captivating stories for their audience.

The satisfaction of solving mysteries and following plots

When we dive into a captivating story, we often feel an intense sense of satisfaction when we manage to solve the mysteries and follow the plots. This feeling is largely due to the activation of our brain's reward system, which is stimulated by solving problems and satisfying our curiosity.

Indeed, when we're confronted with suspenseful situations in a story, our brains go into overdrive, searching for clues and solutions to understand what's going on. This search activates our pleasure and reward centers, encouraging us to keep listening or reading to find the answer.

A striking example of this is the famous TV series "Lost". Viewers were fascinated by the series' complex and mysterious story, desperately searching for clues to understand the mysteries of the island and the characters. This quest created an immersive viewing experience that captivated millions around the world.

Similarly, detective novels and thrillers often have a similar effect on readers, plunging them into a complex investigation and encouraging them to seek answers at every clue or twist.

The satisfaction of solving mysteries and following plots can be extremely gratifying, adding an extra dimension to the reading or viewing experience.

The ability of stories to capture our attention and offer us the satisfaction of solving mysteries and following plots is one of the most fascinating aspects of storytelling.

This immersive experience can transport us into another world and make us forget our own lives for a while, while activating reward mechanisms in our brains that encourage us to keep looking for answers.

6. The cognitive benefits of storytelling: developing emotional and social intelligence

How stories help us understand the motivations and intentions of others

One of the reasons stories are so powerful is that they help us understand the motivations and intentions of others. Stories are often populated by complex characters, whose thoughts and emotions are laid out in great detail. By reading a story, we are invited to put ourselves in the place of the characters and understand their point of view.

This ability to understand the perspectives of others is essential for the development of emotional and social intelligence. When we understand motivations and intentions, we are better equipped to navigate complex social relationships, resolve conflicts and communicate effectively.

Stories can also help us develop empathy. By reading a story, we're invited to put ourselves in the place of the characters and feel what they're feeling. This immersive experience can help us develop our ability to empathize with others in real life.

Stories can also help us understand values and beliefs. By reading a story about a culture different from our own, we are invited to immerse ourselves in a totally new world and explore the values and beliefs that are important to that culture.

An example of the impact of stories on the understanding of motivations and intentions is the series "Breaking Bad". In this series, the main character, Walter White, is a chemistry professor who is diagnosed with terminal cancer. Struggling financially, he decides to go into drug manufacturing to support his family after his death. As the series progresses, we see how Walter's motivations and intentions evolve, and how his actions affect the other characters. This complex exploration of character psychology is one of the reasons why the series has been such a critical and public success.

Stories are an invaluable source of information about the motivations, intentions and values of others. They help us develop our emotional and social intelligence by inviting us to put ourselves in the characters' shoes and understand their point of view.

The importance of storytelling in education and interpersonal communication

Storytelling is a powerful tool for education and interpersonal communication, as it enables complex ideas to be conveyed in an accessible and memorable way. Here are just a few reasons why storytelling is important in these fields:

- **It facilitates understanding**: Stories help to contextualize abstract information, give concrete examples and create mental images that help to better understand concepts. Teachers can use storytelling to make lessons more interesting and students more engaged.

- **It stimulates empathy**: Stories enable us to put ourselves in other people's shoes, to understand their feelings and motivations. This can help students develop their emotional intelligence and communicate better with others.

- **It promotes information retention**: Stories are easier to retain than lists of facts or data. Teachers can use stories to help students memorize key concepts and recall them more easily during exams.

- **It encourages creativity**: Stories are often imaginative and inventive, which can inspire students to be more creative in their work. Teachers can encourage students to create their own stories, or use stories to illustrate key concepts.

- **Facilitates communication**: Stories can be used to improve interpersonal communication, helping people to understand each other better. Stories can help build trust, clarify misunderstandings and resolve conflicts.

Storytelling is a powerful tool for education and interpersonal communication. It can help facilitate understanding, stimulate empathy, foster information retention, encourage creativity and facilitate communication. Teachers, educators, parents and communication professionals can all benefit from using storytelling in their work.

Chapter 3:

The key elements of a compelling story: characters, plot and conflict

In this chapter, I introduce the fundamental elements that make up a compelling story. Touching on character, plot and conflict, as well as other important aspects of storytelling, I guide you through the construction of your own stories, helping you create narratives that touch and engage your audience.

1. Characters: the heart of the story

Creating memorable, engaging characters

To create memorable, engaging characters, it's important to focus on several key aspects. First and foremost, a character must have distinctive traits that make him or her unique and easily identifiable. These traits can be physical, such as scars or tattoos, or psychological, such as strong personality traits or specific life goals. In addition, characters need to be complex, with motivations and emotions that are understandable and authentic.

Another way to create memorable characters is to give them flaws and weaknesses that make them more human and more accessible to the reader or viewer. Characters who are too perfect can seem artificial and uninteresting, while characters who have flaws can seem more authentic and real.

Finally, characters need to be involved in situations that test them and allow them to show their true character. These situations can include conflicts with other characters, external challenges such as natural disasters or battles, or moral dilemmas that test their loyalty and integrity.

To illustrate these points, let's take the example of Harry Potter. Harry is a memorable character because he is instantly recognizable by the lightning bolt scar on his forehead, the result of an attack by the notorious dark wizard Voldemort. He is also complex, with deep-seated motivations to save his friends and defeat Voldemort. In addition, Harry has weaknesses and flaws, not least his tendency to take reckless risks and put himself in danger.

The situations Harry finds himself in are also essential to his character. He faces external challenges such as dangerous magical creatures and powerful enemies, as well as conflicts with friends and foes. Ultimately, these elements combine to create a memorable and endearing character who has become a cultural icon.

In conclusion, to create memorable and engaging characters, it's important to give them distinctive traits, complexity, flaws and put them in situations that allow them to show their true character. These key elements can help characters connect with readers and viewers in deep and meaningful ways, creating captivating and unforgettable stories.

Character archetypes and their role in the story

Character archetypes are recurring patterns in stories that were identified by the famous psychologist Carl Jung and popularized by Joseph Campbell in his book "The Hero with a Thousand Faces". These archetypes, such as the hero, mentor, sage, rebel, clown, etc., are universal characters that resonate with audiences and have been used for centuries in stories to convey messages and values.

The hero archetype, for example, is the main character in the story who must overcome obstacles and challenges to achieve an important goal. The mentor is an older, more experienced character who guides the hero on his quest. The sage is a character of great wisdom and knowledge, who helps the hero find his way. The rebel is a character who challenges authority and established norms, and inspires the hero to stand up for his own convictions.

The use of archetypes in storytelling is important because it enables authors to create characters that are recognizable and easily understood by the audience. Archetypes also enable messages and values to be conveyed more effectively, as they are already embedded in the collective unconscious.

Archetypes can also help authors develop memorable, endearing characters by giving them clear, identifiable personality traits and motivations. Archetypal characters can also be used subversively to create characters who circumvent audience expectations, such as the hero who refuses to follow the path set out for him or the mentor who turns out to be an enemy.

2. The plot: the backbone of the story

How to create a captivating and surprising plot

Plot is the backbone of a compelling story. It is the element that gives life to the characters and drives them to action. To create a captivating and surprising plot, it's important to take several elements into account.

First of all, it's crucial to clearly define the story's main objective. This could be a quest, a mission or a goal to be achieved. The objective must be sufficiently clear and motivating to allow the characters to commit themselves fully to the story.

Next, it's important to add obstacles and twists to keep the reader's interest. Characters need to face challenges that force them to step out of their comfort zone and overcome their fears and doubts. Unexpected twists and turns can also help keep the reader's attention and generate emotion.

You need to create complex, interesting characters with their own motivations and objectives. This creates internal and external conflicts that add depth to the plot.

Finally, it's important to structure the plot according to the principles of dramaturgy. The story must have a clear beginning, middle and end, with moments of tension and resolution.

In storytelling, a compelling plot is essential to maintain the audience's attention and generate emotion. The elements of a good plot can be used to structure a story that has an emotional impact on readers or listeners.

For example, in the film "The Shawshank Redemption", the main objective is the quest for freedom by the main character Andy Dufresne, who is wrongfully imprisoned. In the course of the story, he has to overcome many obstacles, including the brutality of the prison guards and the mistrust of his cellmates. The story is also full of unexpected twists and turns, such as when Andy reveals his escape plan and uses the prison library to dig a tunnel.

Using these plot elements, "The Shawshank Redemption" manages to captivate audiences and evoke emotion. The film has become a cinematic classic, thanks in large part to the captivating, well-structured plot at the heart of the story.

3. Themes: the underlying message

Identifying and exploring universal themes

Storytelling is a technique for conveying a message through a captivating story. Themes are a key element of storytelling, as they add an extra dimension to the story. Themes are the underlying ideas and messages behind the story. They can be universal and appeal to a wide audience, or more specific and aimed at a particular audience.

Identifying themes is an important step in the process of creating a compelling story. Identifying a story's themes involves asking questions about the characters' motivations, the choices they make and the consequences of their actions. Themes can be based on ideas such as love, betrayal, justice, courage, family, freedom, equality, friendship, survival and so on.

Once the themes have been identified, it's important to explore them in the story. Characters and events in the story should reflect the themes in a coherent and meaningful way. Themes can also be reinforced by the dialogue, symbols and metaphors used in the story.

Universal themes are particularly important in storytelling, as they can reach a wide audience and create an emotional bond with readers or viewers. Universal themes are ideas that are relevant to all cultures and all times. For example, love is a universal theme that is present in many stories around the world and in all eras.

By exploring themes within the story, storytelling can help convey important messages to readers or viewers. Stories can be used to raise awareness of social and political issues, teach life lessons or inspire people to take action for positive change.

In conclusion, themes are a key element of storytelling. They add an extra dimension to the story and convey important messages to readers or viewers. By identifying and exploring universal themes, storytelling can reach a wide audience and create an emotional connection with people.

How to convey a message without being sanctimonious

In many stories, the author wishes to convey a message to the reader, without sounding moralistic. For this, storytelling offers an effective technique: suggestion rather than direct statement.

Instead of giving an explicit moral lesson, the author can suggest a message through the events and actions of the characters. For example, a character who faces a difficult decision and makes an ethical choice can convey a message about the value of integrity.

By using realistic, well-developed characters and situations, readers can identify with and become emotionally invested in the story. Messages can then be conveyed in a subtle but powerful way, leaving readers to reflect and draw their own conclusions.

Another common technique is the use of metaphors or allegories to suggest a message. For example, in the famous fable "The Hare and the Tortoise", the tortoise's slowness is a metaphor for perseverance, suggesting that determination and effort are more important than speed and natural talent.

Finally, to convey a message effectively, the author must ensure that the message is in keeping with the plot and the characters. If the message seems forced or artificial, readers may be turned away from the story and lose interest.

Storytelling can convey powerful messages without being moralistic, using techniques of suggestion and metaphor, and ensuring that the message is consistent with the story and the characters.

Chapter 4:

The classic narrative structure: the three-act rule

In this chapter, I discuss the classic three-act narrative structure and explain how it can be used to create a coherent, captivating story. I also present variations and adaptations of this structure for different genres and formats, as well as tips for avoiding common pitfalls.

1. The origin of the three-act structure

The popularity and universality of the three-act structure

The three-act narrative structure is one of the most widely used and popular in the history of storytelling.

It was popularized by the ancient Greeks and used in classic plays such as Shakespeare's, as well as in many modern films and TV series.

This three-act structure is universal, as it follows a pattern that is fundamental to the way humans think about and remember stories. It begins with the introduction of the main character and his or her world, followed by a conflict that creates dramatic tension, ultimately culminating in a resolution that satisfies the audience.

This narrative structure has become popular because it allows a clear, easy-to-follow progression of the story, creating dramatic tension that keeps the audience's attention.

It allows authors to tell complex stories and integrate multiple narrative arcs while remaining coherent and easy to follow.

The three-act structure is a powerful tool for authors of all kinds of stories. It offers a universal way of telling compelling stories that capture the imagination and emotions of readers or viewers.

2. The first act: setting up

The first act is the first third of the three-act structure, also known as the exposition act. Its main purpose is to set up the elements of the story: characters, world, plot and themes.

Here are some key elements of the set-up in the first act:

- **Introducing the main characters and their world**: This is the opportunity to introduce the heroes, antagonists and secondary characters who play an important role in the story. Characters must be sufficiently well defined for the audience to identify with them and understand their motivations.

- **Defining the plot**: The plot must be introduced clearly and concisely in the first act. The stakes of the story must be established, as well as the obstacles the characters will have to overcome.

- **Themes**: The main themes of the story should be introduced in the first act. Themes can be explicit or implicit, but they must be clearly established so that the audience can understand the story's underlying message.

- **Setting tone and style**: The first act is also an opportunity to set the tone and style of the story. Is it a light comedy or a dark drama? Tone and style must be consistent throughout the story.

- **Creating a hook**: The first act must capture the audience's attention and encourage them to continue watching or reading the story. To do this, it's often helpful to create an intriguing hook or situation that keeps the audience on the edge of their seats.

In short, the first act is crucial in setting up all the key elements of the story.

Once these elements are in place, the story can fully develop in the second act.

3. The second act: development

The second act is the central part of the three-act narrative structure, where the plot develops and the characters must overcome obstacles to reach their goal. This development can be divided into several key stages:

1. **Confrontation**: characters face challenges and obstacles that hinder their progress towards their goal.

2. **The revelation**: crucial information is revealed that changes the plot and the perception of the characters and the audience.

3. **Preparation**: the characters prepare to overcome the plot's main obstacle.

4. **The point of no return**: a major event occurs that irrevocably changes the course of history.

5. **The climax**: the moment of maximum tension when the characters face the main obstacle.

6. **Resolution**: the characters overcome the obstacle and reach their goal.

In the second act, the audience becomes more invested in the story and the characters, and feels a sense of progression and urgency. This is a crucial step in maintaining the audience's interest until the end of the story.

Storytelling is fundamental to bringing this three-act narrative structure to life, creating memorable characters, compelling plots and universal themes. Here are a few examples of stories that make effective use of the second act:

- **The Lord of the Rings**: The development of the plot revolves around Frodo's quest to destroy the One Ring, with a series of challenges and obstacles standing in his way.

- **Harry Potter**: In every book in the series, the second act follows the development of the plot around the discovery of a new element in the world of magic, while highlighting the obstacles and challenges Harry and his friends must overcome to achieve their goal.

- **Star Wars**: In the original trilogy, plot development centered on Luke Skywalker's quest to defeat the Empire and save the galaxy, with a series of battles and obstacles standing in his way.

By using engaging characters, universal themes and captivating narrative elements, these stories succeed in creating a stimulating and emotionally engaging second act.

4. The third act: resolution

The third act of the classic narrative structure is that of resolution, also known as the denouement. In this part of the story, the conflicts that have been established throughout the second act must be resolved. This is the moment when the protagonist must face up to the consequences of his or her choices and actions, and the story reaches its climax.

To create a captivating resolution, it is important to consider the following elements:

- **The resolution must be satisfying for the audience**. This means that all plot elements must be resolved logically and convincingly, without leaving any unresolved questions or narrative threads.

- **The protagonist must have made significant progress**. The main character must have learned something or undergone a significant transformation during the course of the story. This may be in response to plot events, or through relationships with other characters.

- **The resolution must be credible**. The events that occur must be logical and consistent with what has been established earlier in the story. Characters must not act inconsistently or out of character to resolve conflicts.

- **The resolution must be emotionally satisfying**. Readers should feel some catharsis or emotional relief at the end of the story. This can be achieved by creating a happy ending, leaving a lasting impression, or by having the main character accomplish something important or significant.

Examples of satisfying and memorable resolutions in literature include the ending of Harper Lee's "To Kill a Mockingbird", where the main character Atticus Finch must face the injustice of the American justice system, but remains a role model for his community. Another memorable ending is that of George Orwell's "1984", where the main character Winston Smith finally accepts the totalitarian regime he had previously fought against.

In films, resolution can take the form of the protagonist's victory in "Rocky", or the final revelation in "The Usual Suspects". In video games, resolution can be the completion of the main quest in "The Legend of Zelda: Breath of the Wild", or the revelation of the truth about the story in "Bioshock Infinite".

The third act of the classic narrative structure is crucial to providing a satisfying ending to the story. A credible, emotionally satisfying resolution will help leave a lasting impression on the audience and reinforce the power of storytelling.

5. What's the point of mastering the three acts?

Mastering the three acts of the classic narrative structure is essential for storytelling, as it enables you to tell a captivating, coherent story. This structure maintains the audience's attention by creating narrative rhythm and tension.

By mastering this narrative structure, authors can create captivating and memorable stories, evoking emotions in readers or viewers. Brands can also use this structure to tell their story more effectively and create an emotional connection with their target audience.

Part 2:

Storytelling in marketing

Chapter 5:

Brand storytelling: giving your company a soul

In this chapter, I discuss the importance of storytelling for brands and how it can give your company a soul. I present the various steps involved in building a captivating and authentic brand story, focusing on mission, vision, origin story, values and corporate culture, as well as tone and style of communication.

1. The importance of storytelling for brands

How stories reinforce brand identity and personality

Stories are a powerful way for brands to communicate their identity and personality to consumers. By telling stories, brands can create an emotional connection with their target audience and give them a reason to engage with the brand. Here are just some of the ways stories can reinforce a brand's identity and personality:

1. **Highlight brand values**: By telling stories that illustrate the brand's values, consumers can better understand what the brand stands for and what it stands for. For example, if a clothing brand focuses on sustainability and ethics, it could tell a story about how its clothes are made from sustainable and eco-friendly materials, highlighting the brand's values.

2. **Creating a distinct brand personality**: Stories can help create a distinct brand personality that stands out from the competition. For example, if a fast-food brand wants to differentiate itself by focusing on the customer experience, it could tell stories about how it creates memorable experiences for its customers, highlighting the brand's personality.

3. **Strengthen the emotional connection with consumers**: Stories can help establish an emotional connection with consumers, giving them a reason to engage with the brand. By telling stories that evoke positive emotions, consumers can feel more connected and engaged with the brand.

4. **Humanizing the brand**: Stories can help humanize the brand by making it more

accessible and showing that there are real people behind it. By telling stories about the people who work for the brand, or the people who have benefited from the brand's products or services, consumers can better understand the brand and feel closer to it.

By using storytelling to reinforce their brand's identity and personality, companies can create a more memorable and engaging experience for their target audience. Consumers will remember the brand more easily and be more likely to engage with it in the future.

The benefits of storytelling for customer engagement and loyalty

Storytelling is a powerful tool for creating an emotional bond between a brand and its customers, which can foster customer engagement and loyalty. Indeed, stories can help evoke emotions and feelings in customers, who will then identify with the brand and feel concerned by what it offers.

Here are just a few of the benefits of storytelling for customer engagement and loyalty:

- **Storytelling can help create a sense of community**: By telling a story that's in tune with the brand's values, it's possible to create a community of loyal customers who feel connected to one another. This community can then become a place of exchange and sharing, fostering customer engagement.

- **Storytelling can help personalize the customer experience**: Using storytelling, a brand can create a story that fits each customer and makes them feel unique and special. This can help strengthen the emotional bond between brand and customer, promoting engagement and loyalty.

- **Storytelling can help create an emotional attachment to the brand**: By telling a story that evokes positive emotions, a brand can create an emotional attachment in its customers. This attachment can then translate into greater loyalty, as customers will be more inclined to remain loyal to a brand that evokes positive emotions.

- **Storytelling can help create a strong brand image**: By telling a story that reflects the brand's values and personality, it's possible to strengthen the brand image and make it more memorable. A strong brand image can then help build customer loyalty, as they will be more inclined to remain loyal to a brand with a strong personality.

By using storytelling effectively, a brand can therefore create a strong emotional bond with its customers, which can foster engagement and loyalty. It is therefore important for brands to understand the importance of storytelling and use it strategically to reinforce their identity and personality.

3. The origin story: your brand's roots

Key elements of a convincing origin story

A compelling origin story is essential to lend credibility and authenticity to your brand. Here are the key elements for creating one:

Authenticity

The origin story must be truthful and reflect the brand's core values.

Emotion

An origin story must be emotionally powerful, captivating the audience's attention and interest. It must elicit an emotional response from listeners or readers.

Uniqueness

The story must stand out from those of other brands in the same sector. It must have a unique difference, a unique value proposition and a story to tell that can't be imitated.

Relevance

The story must be relevant to the target audience. It must reflect their values and interests.

Simplicity

The story must be simple, easy to understand and remember. It must be easy to tell and share.

Continuity

The story must be consistent with the brand and the key messages it wishes to convey. It must be integrated into the company's overall communications strategy.

To illustrate these key elements, let's take the example of cosmetics brand Lush. Their origin story dates back to 1995, when founder Mark Constantine decided to create a natural, handmade cosmetics company. This idea grew out of his experience in the cosmetics industry, where he had worked for years and seen first-hand the negative effects of synthetic ingredients on the skin and the environment.

For Lush, the origin story is a key element of their brand. They tell this story with passion and conviction, and it's reflected in every aspect of their business, from the way they choose their ingredients, to the way they present their products.

Here are some key elements of their compelling origin story:

- **A cause**: Mark Constantine's passion for natural cosmetics and his desire to make a difference in the industry were the driving forces behind the creation of Lush. This passion is at the heart of the brand's history and is conveyed through their communications.

- **An artisanal approach**: Lush was founded on the idea of making quality products by hand, using fresh, natural ingredients. This artisanal approach is at the heart of their brand identity and origin story.

- **A vision**: Lush has a clear vision of their place in the cosmetics industry. They are here to make a positive change, offering natural alternatives to synthetic products and promoting sustainable practices.

By telling their origin story in a compelling way, Lush has managed to stand out in an industry saturated with big brands. Their commitment to quality, naturalness and the environment is clear to consumers, who are often willing to pay a little more to support a brand that shares their values.

A compelling origin story is a key element in giving your company a soul and reinforcing your brand identity.

By using the key elements mentioned above, you can create a story that arouses interest and emotion, while being consistent with your overall communication strategy.

4. Corporate values and culture: the soul of your brand

How to define and communicate your corporate values

In an increasingly competitive market, it's important for a company to differentiate itself from its competitors and develop a strong brand. One of the most effective ways of achieving this is to clearly define and communicate the company's values and culture.

Defining the company's values should be a fundamental step in the marketing strategy, as it forms the basis of brand communication. Values must be aligned with the company's mission and vision, as well as with customers' expectations and aspirations.

Storytelling can play a key role in communicating corporate values. By telling stories that illustrate the company's values in action, customers can connect emotionally with the brand and identify with the values it represents.

When defining corporate values, it is important to take into account the opinions and expectations of stakeholders, including customers, employees and shareholders. Values must be clearly defined and communicated at all levels of the company, to ensure consistency in brand communication.

Once values have been defined, it's important to put them into action. Customers are more likely to trust a company that practises what it preaches. By showing how values are integrated into the company's products, services and processes, it can reinforce customer trust and loyalty.

You need to communicate values consistently and strategically. Storytelling can be used to tell stories that illustrate how values are integrated into the business, and to show the benefits to customers of doing business with a company that shares their values.

Corporate values and culture are key to developing a strong brand and differentiating from competitors. The definition and communication of values must be aligned with the company's mission and vision, and communicated consistently and strategically at all levels of the organization. Storytelling can play a key role in communicating these values in action.

The importance of corporate culture in brand storytelling

Corporate culture plays an essential role in brand storytelling, as it is the very essence of the company's soul. It encompasses the values, beliefs, attitudes and behaviors that govern interactions within the company. It is therefore crucial to the way the company presents itself to the public.

Brand storytelling is a technique that enables companies to tell a story of their own, creating an emotional connection with their target audience. To succeed in this endeavor, it's crucial that the story told is consistent with the brand's corporate culture. Stories must reflect the values and beliefs embedded in the company. Customers want to know what the company stands for and believes in before they decide to buy its products or services.

Brands that successfully integrate their corporate culture into their storytelling can create a more meaningful and authentic brand experience for their audience. Customers have a strong propensity to engage with brands that share their values and beliefs, and reflect them in their communication and behavior. By focusing on corporate culture, companies can bring their brand to life and offer a more human and authentic experience to their audience.

5. Heroes and brand ambassadors: the faces of your story

The importance of brand ambassadors

Brand ambassadors play a crucial role in corporate storytelling, embodying the brand's values, image and personality. They can be company employees, public figures or loyal consumers who share their experience with the brand.

The use of brand ambassadors can reinforce brand credibility, as they provide social proof by testifying to their positive experience with the brand. They can also help to humanize the brand by giving the company a face and a voice.

What's more, brand ambassadors can help reach new audiences by sharing their experience with their own network of contacts and encouraging them to discover the brand in turn.

It's important to choose the right brand ambassadors based on their compatibility with the company's values and their ability to embody the brand's identity in an authentic way. It's also important to ensure that they have a strong presence on social networks and an engaged audience to maximize the impact of their testimonial.

The storytelling of your ambassadors can very well be linked to the storytelling of your brand. If the story of one of your ambassadors is compelling, why not link it to your brand story?

How to identify and promote your brand ambassadors

To identify and value your brand ambassadors, it's important to understand their role in your brand story. Brand ambassadors are the people who embody your company's values and talk about them to those around them, be they customers, employees or partners.

Here are a few steps to identify and promote your brand ambassadors:

1. **Identify people who are passionate about your brand**: This could be loyal customers, committed employees or partners who share your values. You can use surveys, polls or analytics to find these people.

2. **Identify people with a strong presence on social networks**: Influencers, bloggers

or people with a strong presence on social networks can be good ambassadors for your brand.

3. **Encourage and reward your brand ambassadors**: Offer them exclusive benefits, gifts or rewards for their commitment to your brand. This can encourage them to tell their friends and family, and strengthen their relationship with your company.

4. **Use their testimonials to reinforce your brand storytelling**: The testimonials and personal stories of your ambassadors can be used in your brand storytelling to reinforce your company's credibility and emotional connection with your audience.

By valuing your brand ambassadors, you can strengthen your company's credibility and improve your relationship with your customers, employees and partners. It can also help strengthen your brand storytelling by using their testimonials and personal stories to give your company an authentic, human voice.

Chapter 6:

Examples of successful storytelling by major brands

In this chapter, I present examples of major brands that have succeeded in creating impeccable storytelling, focusing on their origin story, mission, vision, and iconic campaigns. These examples illustrate how successful storytelling can reinforce a brand's identity and create a strong emotional bond with consumers.

1. Apple: innovation and simplicity at the service of the user

Apple's origin story and the impact of Steve Jobs

Let me tell you about Apple's origin story, which is closely linked to its successful storytelling.

The Apple story began in 1976, when Steve Jobs and Steve Wozniak created the first personal computer in Jobs' parents' garage. At the time, computers were reserved for large corporations and government institutions. However, Jobs and Wozniak saw untapped potential and decided to create an affordable personal computer for everyone. They created the first personal computer, the Apple I, which was revolutionary for its time.

However, Apple's history is not limited to technological innovation. It is also marked by the charismatic personality of its co-founder, Steve Jobs. He was known for his unique vision, creativity, perfectionism and passion for design. Jobs succeeded in creating a corporate culture focused on innovation, creativity and simplicity. This culture was integrated into the company's DNA and has remained a key element of its storytelling.

Apple's storytelling has been built around these key elements of its origin story. The brand has captivated consumers by creating innovative products that have transformed people's lives. It has also created a myth around its founders, in particular Steve Jobs, presenting them as visionaries who changed the world. The company has also incorporated Apple's history into its advertising, using slogans such as "Think Different" to illustrate its culture of innovation and creativity.

By using key elements of its original story, Apple has created a strong, consistent brand identity that has become a benchmark in the technology industry.

Consumers have come to associate the Apple brand with innovation, simplicity and elegant design, and have become loyal to the brand.

Apple's history and successful storytelling have been key to its success. It has captured the imagination of consumers by creating products that have changed their lives, while creating a corporate culture focused on innovation, creativity and simplicity. Apple has used its history to create a strong, consistent brand identity that has become a benchmark, setting the brand apart from its competitors.

The values and vision that shape Apple's storytelling

Apple is a company that has succeeded in forging a strong brand image by focusing on key values. At the heart of its philosophy are innovation, simplicity and user experience. These values are reflected throughout the company's storytelling.

Innovation has been the driving force behind the company since its inception. Steve Jobs was a man who was always ahead of his time. He launched numerous products that revolutionized the technology industry. Jobs' vision was to create products that would change people's lives. This passion for innovation is still present at Apple today, as evidenced by the regular launches of new products and services.

Simplicity is another of the company's core values. Apple has always sought to simplify technology and make it accessible to everyone. The company's philosophy is that technology should be easy to use, effortless and intuitive. This vision is reflected in the design of their products, which are renowned for their simplicity and elegance.

User experience is also a core value for Apple. The company believes that technology should improve people's lives and make everyday tasks simpler and more enjoyable. The company places users at the center of its storytelling, helping them to understand how their products can help them live their lives more effectively.

Apple's storytelling is built around these key values. The company uses stories to convey its vision and share its enthusiasm for innovation, simplicity and user experience. Apple's advertising campaigns often feature stories of people using their products to simplify their lives or accomplish tasks they never thought possible. The stories are told in a simple, straightforward way, in keeping with the company's philosophy.

Apple's storytelling is also based on a strong visual aesthetic. The company often uses simple, uncluttered images to showcase its products, and the design of its ads is often minimalist. This helps reinforce the image of simplicity and elegance the company wishes to convey.

Finally, Apple's storytelling is also based on clear, simple language. Advertising messages are often succinct and easy to understand, enabling the company to reach a wider audience.

Apple's core values of innovation, simplicity and user experience are at the heart of the company's storytelling. The stories the company tells through its advertising and communications are simple, visually appealing and easy to understand. This approach helps to reinforce the company's brand image and make it more accessible to consumers.

2. Nike: inspiration and emancipation through sport

Nike's mission and values

Nike is one of the world's best-known brands, thanks to its remarkable history and storytelling. Nike's mission is to "bring inspiration and innovation to athletes everywhere", which has inspired many of the brand's advertising campaigns and events. Nike's values are centered on innovation, inspiration and empowerment through sport.

Nike was founded in 1964 by Bill Bowerman and Phil Knight, under the name Blue Ribbon Sports. At the time, Bowerman was a track coach at the University of Oregon, and Knight was one of his runners. Together, they formed a company to import high-quality Japanese running shoes to the United States. In 1971, they renamed their company Nike, after the Greek goddess of victory.

Over the years, Nike has become one of the world's leading sports brands, known for its innovation, design and ability to inspire athletes and sports enthusiasts alike. Nike has also pioneered brand storytelling in sports, creating iconic advertising campaigns that have captivated millions of people around the world.

Nike's storytelling draws on these values to inspire consumers to push their limits and surpass themselves. The brand seeks to create an emotional relationship with consumers by addressing their desire to surpass themselves and achieve their goals, whatever they may be. By using renowned athletes, encouraging messages and inspiring stories, Nike creates a strong and engaging identity for its brand.

A prime example of Nike's storytelling is its "Just Do It" campaign. This campaign has become emblematic for the brand, as it encourages people to step out of their comfort zone and challenge themselves not only in their sporting activities, but also in their everyday lives. The "Just Do It" campaign addresses everyone's aspiration to be better, stronger, braver and more determined.

Nike's mission and values are reflected in its storytelling, which seeks to inspire consumers to reach their full potential through sport and determination. Nike's storytelling shows that the emotional engagement of consumers is essential to establishing a lasting connection with a brand.

Nike's iconic advertising campaigns and storytelling

Nike is a company that has turned storytelling into an art form and an effective marketing weapon. The brand is known for its iconic advertising campaigns, which combine creativity, emotional power and visual impact. Each of these campaigns tells a story that goes beyond simply selling a product, conveying an emotion, an idea, an attitude.

Nike's most iconic advertising campaigns include "Just Do It", "Find Your Greatness", "Unlimited You", "Dream Crazy" and "The Chance". Each of these campaigns has its own message and its own story.

- **The "Just Do It" campaign, which** I mentioned earlier, was launched in 1988, with the famous slogan "Just Do It". The campaign aimed to inspire consumers to be more active and achieve their goals, whatever their fitness level or age. The campaign was an immediate success, positioning Nike as a brand that encourages self-accomplishment and ambition.

- **The "Find Your Greatness" campaign**, launched in 2012, promoted the idea that anyone can achieve greatness, whatever their physical condition or skill level. The campaign was a tribute to everyday athletes, who work hard to achieve their goals and are often overlooked in a world focused on exceptional performance. The campaign emphasized the importance of perseverance, motivation and training to achieve one's goals.

- **The "Unlimited You" campaign**, launched in 2016, highlighted the importance of pushing your limits and exploring your potential. The campaign featured athletes from all walks of life, who overcame obstacles and achieved their dreams through determination and perseverance. The campaign was a call to action for all those striving to reach their maximum potential.

- **The "Dream Crazy" campaign**, launched in 2018, highlighted the importance of following your dreams, even when it seems impossible. The campaign featured the participation of Colin Kaepernick, an American soccer player who protested against police violence and racial inequality by kneeling during the national anthem. The campaign underlined the importance of freedom of expression and the fight against prejudice and stereotypes.

- **The "The Chance" campaign**, launched in 2010, was a global campaign aimed at discovering young soccer talent through regional selections and competitions. The campaign was an opportunity for young players to realize their dream of becoming soccer professionals and joining the Nike family.

All these advertising campaigns have one thing in common: they all have a story to tell. They have all used the power of storytelling to convey a strong, inspiring message.

3. Coca-Cola: sharing happiness and conviviality

Coca-Cola's history and development

Coca-Cola is an American brand created in 1886 by pharmacist John Pemberton. At first, the drink was marketed as a remedy for stomach aches and headaches. But its sweet taste soon won consumers over, and Coca-Cola became a popular drink the world over.

Over the years, Coca-Cola has evolved into an iconic brand, associated with values of conviviality, happiness and sharing. The brand has succeeded in renewing itself by offering new products and adapting its communications to changes in society.

Coca-Cola has also created a strong storytelling style, highlighting moments of conviviality and sharing through memorable advertising campaigns.

Coca-Cola has also adapted its storytelling to environmental issues, launching awareness campaigns on waste reduction and environmental protection.

It's an iconic brand that has evolved over the years, while retaining its identity and its values of conviviality and sharing. Coca-Cola's storytelling, based on these values, has helped make the brand a global reference.

The campaigns and stories that have shaped Coca-Cola storytelling

Right from the start in 1886, Coca-Cola founder John Pemberton set out to create a refreshing, invigorating drink that would spread joy and good cheer. This idea was soon taken up by the Coca-Cola Company, which developed a communications strategy based on innovative advertising campaigns and memorable stories.

One of Coca-Cola's most famous advertising campaigns is undoubtedly "Hilltop" in 1971. This campaign was created to promote a song entitled "I'd Like to Buy the World a Coke", which conveys a message of unity, friendship and sharing. The ad shows people of different cultures and nationalities gathering on a hill to drink a Coca-Cola and sing together. The campaign became emblematic of the brand and marked the beginning of storytelling in Coca-Cola marketing.

Coca-Cola has also adapted to changes in society and the media by developing stories that resonate with today's consumers. For example, the "Share a Coca-Cola" campaign launched in 2011 was a huge success, personalizing bottles and cans with popular first names. The campaign encouraged consumers to share a Coca-Cola with friends and family, reinforcing the brand's core values of friendship and sharing.

Finally, Coca-Cola has created inspiring stories by featuring athletes and celebrities in its advertising campaigns. For example, the "Reasons to Believe" campaign features stories of people who have overcome obstacles to achieve their dreams, highlighting values of optimism and perseverance.

Through its advertising campaigns and stories, the brand has succeeded in conveying positive, universal values, creating a strong, enduring brand image. The brand has reinvented itself over the years, using storytelling to stay relevant and connected with its audience.

4. Airbnb: a more welcoming, connected world

Airbnb's origin story and vision

The Airbnb story begins in 2007, when two San Francisco roommates, Brian Chesky and Joe Gebbia, came up with the idea of renting out air mattresses in their apartment for visitors to the San Francisco Design Conference. They quickly realized that this could become a viable business and created Airbnb. The name was born from the idea of offering a service that would allow people to sleep on an inflatable mattress, air (Air), and share their living space (bnb, for bed and breakfast). The company's goal was to enable people to find unique and authentic accommodations around the world, while offering a more personal and connected travel experience.

Airbnb's vision is to "create a world where anyone can feel at home anywhere". This vision is founded on the idea that travel can bring people together and foster mutual understanding. By offering homestays, Airbnb offers travelers the opportunity to live like a local and connect with the local community. This can help break down cultural barriers and promote mutual understanding and respect.

Airbnb's storytelling is based on the belief that travel is a personal experience and that accommodations are more than just places to sleep. The company highlights the unique travel experiences and stories of hosts and travelers who have used Airbnb to find authentic accommodations. Airbnb's advertising campaigns often feature travelers who have had memorable experiences using the service, such as a family who rented a castle in Scotland or a couple who spent a night in a cabin in Alaska.

Airbnb's origin story, then, is that of two roommates who came up with an ingenious idea to rent out air mattresses. The company's vision is to connect people through travel by offering unique and authentic accommodations. Airbnb's storytelling emphasizes unique travel experiences and the stories of hosts and travelers, allowing the company to differentiate itself from other travel services and create a community of loyal travelers.

Campaigns and initiatives that illustrate Airbnb storytelling

Airbnb is a brand that has exploited the advantages of storytelling to set itself apart in the marketplace. The advertising campaigns and initiatives launched by the brand all have one thing in common: they emphasize the notion of community, open-mindedness, and the discovery of new cultures.

Here are a few examples:

- **"Is Mankind?"** : This campaign, launched in 2017, is centered on the idea that we have more in common than differences. It features people from different backgrounds, cultures, religions, sexualities, etc., sharing their vision of welcome and open-mindedness. The campaign video also features Airbnb hosts sharing their experience and passion for hospitality.

- **"We Accept"**: this campaign, launched in 2017, is a direct response to Donald Trump's migration policy. It aims to show that the brand is open to all travelers, regardless of their origin or religion. The message is clear: at Airbnb, everyone is welcome.

- **"Airbnb Experiences"**: this initiative launched in 2016 enables Airbnb hosts to offer local activities to their guests, ranging from local cuisine to mountain hiking. The initiative promotes the idea that travel isn't just about hotels and tourist sites, but can be an opportunity to discover a culture from the inside out.

- **"Night At"**: This initiative enables people to stay in unusual places, such as an airplane, a tree house, a castle, and so on. This initiative promotes the idea of adventure and the discovery of unique places, and is in line with the brand's philosophy of hospitality and open-mindedness.

These examples illustrate Airbnb's ability to create inspiring stories and touch consumers' emotions. By emphasizing values such as open-mindedness, discovery and community, Airbnb has created a strong and memorable brand image. This demonstrates the importance of creativity and innovation in brand storytelling.

5. Patagonia: environmental commitment and sustainability

Patagonia's mission and values

The Patagonia brand is known for its environmental commitment and sustainability philosophy, which is reflected throughout its storytelling. Its mission is to "build the best product, cause no unnecessary harm, use business to inspire and implement solutions to the environmental crisis". The brand is deeply committed to environmental protection and believes that companies have a responsibility to the planet.

The brand's values are closely linked to its mission, and the brand emphasizes its transparency, commitment and passion for the environment. Patagonia believes in the need to protect the planet's wild places, and encourages its customers to take action to protect the environment.

Patagonia's storytelling is based on stories of exploration and outdoor adventure, as well as its commitment to the environment. The brand's advertising campaigns feature adventurers, athletes and environmental activists who share the brand's passion for nature and adventure. Patagonia's stories also reflect its mission and values, encouraging people to get out and discover the wonders of nature, while taking care of the planet.

In addition, the brand has put in place numerous initiatives to support its environmental commitment, such as its "Worn Wear" program, which encourages customers to repair their Patagonia garments rather than throw them away, or its commitment to donating 1% of sales to environmental organizations.

Patagonia's storytelling is based on its mission and environmental values, which are highlighted in all its advertising campaigns and initiatives. The brand strives to raise awareness of the importance of protecting the environment, while encouraging people to get out and enjoy nature.

Campaigns and concrete actions that strengthen Patagonia's storytelling

Patagonia is a company that has always aimed to preserve the environment and encourage sustainability. This is clearly reflected in their brand storytelling. Here are some of Patagonia's concrete campaigns and actions that illustrate this mission and reinforce their storytelling:

- **"Don't buy this jacket"**: In 2011, Patagonia launched an advertising campaign inviting consumers to think before they buy new clothes and consider the environmental impact of their choices. The campaign featured a Patagonia jacket with the slogan "Don't buy this jacket" and encouraged people to repair their existing clothes rather than buy new ones.

- **Recycling programs**: Patagonia has set up several recycling programs to help consumers give a second life to their clothing. They also offer advice on how to maintain and repair garments to extend their lifespan.

- **The Environmental Defense Fund**: Patagonia has established an Environmental Defense Fund that donates millions of dollars each year to environmental advocacy groups around the world. Grants support projects to protect wild lands and waters, combat climate change and promote sustainable agriculture.

- **Commercials and documentaries**: Patagonia has produced several commercials and documentaries to highlight their environmental commitment. For example, the documentary series "The Footprint Chronicles" follows the production journey of some of Patagonia's garments, highlighting the environmental and social challenges facing the company.

All these campaigns and concrete actions by Patagonia clearly illustrate their mission and values when it comes to the environment and sustainability. They don't just tell their story, they live it and put it into action. This reinforces the credibility of their storytelling and sets them apart from their competitors.

Chapter 7:

Social media and storytelling: building a community around your story

In this chapter, I discuss the importance of social media in modern storytelling and how to build a community around your story. I present tips for adapting your storytelling to different social media platforms and creating engaging content. Finally, I discuss strategies for maintaining a close relationship with your audience and encouraging their participation and sharing of your story.

1. The importance of social media in modern storytelling

The reach and influence of social media on the public

Social media have radically changed the way people communicate, share and access information. They have enabled greater reach and influence for brands and individuals who want to tell their story.

Social media platforms such as Facebook, Twitter, Instagram, TikTok and LinkedIn enable brands to reach a global audience quickly and effectively.

Social media have enabled greater interactivity and engagement between brands and their audiences. Consumers can interact directly with brands, commenting on and sharing their content, and even co-creating stories with them. This enables brands to connect more authentically and personally with their audience, building a community of people who share the same values and interests.

Social media has become a key element of modern storytelling, enabling brands to spread their message in a creative and engaging way. Stories are shared in the form of photos, videos, text and graphics, to create visually appealing, easily shareable content. Social media allows brands to measure and analyze the impact of their storytelling, tracking likes, shares, comments and interactions. This enables brands to understand how their audience reacts to their content and adjust accordingly.

Social media therefore have an immense influence on the way brands tell their story and communicate with their audience. They enable greater reach, interactivity and engagement, while offering valuable analysis of results. Storytelling on social media is therefore a key element of any modern, effective marketing strategy.

Social media opportunities for storytelling

Social media offer many opportunities for creative and engaging storytelling. Indeed, brands can use different formats to share their story, such as photos, videos, stories, lives, posts, etc. What's more, social media enables direct interaction with audiences and the creation of a community around a brand's story.

Here are just a few examples of the storytelling opportunities offered by social media:

Visuals

Images and videos are highly effective ways of telling a story visually. Brands can use professional-quality images or videos to capture the audience's attention and tell their story in a more dynamic way. Visuals must be carefully chosen to reflect the brand's identity and the message it wishes to convey.

Testimonials

Testimonials from satisfied customers are a great way to tell a brand's story through the eyes of its customers. Brands can use written testimonials, videos or even audio recordings to share their customers' experiences and show the positive impact of their products or services.

Hashtags

Hashtags are effective ways of generating engagement around a brand's story. Brands can create customized hashtags for their advertising campaigns, or encourage their audiences to use specific hashtags to share their experiences with the brand's products or services. This creates a community around the brand and makes it easier for new audiences to discover its story.

Stories live

Lives on social networks are a great way to tell a story in an authentic and spontaneous way. Brands can use lives to go behind the scenes of their business, showcase their employees or even organize live events to interact directly with their audience.

User-generated content

User-generated content, such as photos or videos of customers using the brand's products or services, is a great way to tell the brand's story through the eyes of its customers. Brands can encourage their customers to share their experiences with specific hashtags or enter contests to win prizes.

Social media offer many opportunities for creative and engaging storytelling. Brands can use different formats and tools to share their story and create a community around their brand. Storytelling is essential to connect emotionally with audiences, and social media is a great way to do this in an innovative and effective way.

2. Adapt your storytelling to different social media platforms

The specific features of each platform and how to use them to tell your story

Of course, the different social media platforms each have their own specificities in terms of format, audience and tone. By adapting your storytelling to each platform, you can reach your audience more effectively and engage your community more fully. Here are some specifics of each platform and how to use them to tell your story:

- **Facebook**: Facebook is ideal for telling longer, more complex stories, such as customer testimonials or stories from the life of the company. Videos are also very effective

127

on Facebook, especially live videos and stories. Use attractive visuals and clear captions to maximize the impact of your message.

- **Instagram**: Instagram is a visual platform, so use high-quality images and videos to tell your story. Use relevant hashtags to reach new audiences, and use inspiring, engaging captions to encourage users to interact with your content. Instagram stories are also a great way to tell ephemeral stories and create a more personal relationship with your audience.

- **Twitter**: Twitter is all about text and brevity, so use short, concise messages to tell your story. Use relevant hashtags to reach new audiences, and retweet tweets from your community to encourage interaction and engagement.

- **LinkedIn**: LinkedIn is a professional platform, so use a more formal, business-focused tone to tell your story. Use longer posts to share more complex stories, but also short, inspiring stories to engage your audience.

- **YouTube**: YouTube is ideal for telling stories through longer, more elaborate videos. Use high-quality visuals and appropriate soundtracks to add depth to your story. Video descriptions and titles should be clear and concise to reach your target audience.

By adapting your storytelling to each platform, you can reach new audiences and further engage your community. By keeping in mind the specifics of each platform, you can tell your story more effectively and create deeper relationships with your audience.

Tips for creating engaging social media content

To create engaging, social media-friendly content, there are several tips to follow:

1. **Know your target audience**: before creating content, it's important to know the expectations and needs of your target audience, so you can adapt your content accordingly.

2. **Use attractive visuals**: images and videos are more engaging than text alone. Use quality images and short, punchy videos to grab your audience's attention.

3. **Telling stories**: use storytelling to tell stories that capture your audience's attention. Stories should be linked to your brand's values and mission.

4. **Use relevant hashtags**: hashtags allow you to extend the reach of your content and reach a wider audience. Use hashtags that are relevant to your content and industry.

5. **Interact with your audience**: social media allow you to interact directly with your audience. Respond to comments and private messages to create a relationship of trust with your audience.

6. **Vary content formats**: social media offer a wide variety of content formats. Use different formats (images, videos, infographics, carousels...) to diversify your content and reach a wider audience.

By following these tips, you can create engaging, social-media-friendly content, strengthen your storytelling and build a community around your brand.

3. Build and maintain a community around your story

Strategies for creating an emotional bond with your audience on social media

Social media are an excellent way for brands to tell their story and create an engaged community around their mission and values. However, to succeed in creating an emotional connection with your audience, it's important to use effective strategies.

The first strategy is to feature testimonials and personal stories from customers or users of the brand. This shows that the brand is genuine and cares about its customers. Testimonials can be shared in the form of videos, photos, or even posts on social networks.

The second strategy is to use events or initiatives to engage your community. For example, the brand can organize a contest or challenge to encourage users to share their experience with the brand, or create physical events to enable the community to meet and exchange.

The third strategy is to use social networks to disseminate strong messages in line with the brand's mission and values. This can be done through social network posts, videos, infographics or podcasts. It's important that the content is visually appealing and easy to consume, to capture the audience's attention.

Finally, to encourage participation and sharing of your story, it's essential to interact with your community. This can be done through replying to comments, sharing user posts, or even creating hashtags to allow your community to participate in a conversation around the brand. It's also important to thank and value community members for their engagement.

To build and maintain an engaged community around your story on social media, it's essential to feature testimonials and personal stories, use events or initiatives to engage your community, deliver strong messages in line with the brand's mission and values, and interact with your community.

Part 3:

Master the art of storytelling

Chapter 8:

Finding the right story: brainstorming and ideation techniques

In this chapter, I present different techniques for finding the story that resonates with your audience. I cover the steps involved in understanding your audience, generating ideas through brainstorming, using archetypes and universal themes, and drawing on existing resources to fuel your creativity. Finally, I offer advice on how to choose and refine the story that best suits your objectives.

1. Understand your audience and their needs

How to identify your audience's problems and expectations

To find the story that will resonate with your audience, it's essential to understand their problems and expectations. Indeed, to create an emotional bond with your audience, it's important to show that you understand their needs and concerns.

To identify your audience's problems and expectations, it's important to conduct in-depth research into your market and target audience. There are a number of techniques you can use to achieve this.

Analysis of demographic data

This method involves analyzing the characteristics of your target audience, such as age, gender, place of residence, profession, etc. This information can help you better understand your audience's needs and expectations. This information can help you better understand your audience's needs and expectations.

Surveys and polls

You can use surveys and polls to gather your audience's opinions and expectations directly. Surveys can be conducted online or offline, and you can offer a reward or gift to encourage participants.

Analysis of conversations on social networks

Social networks are a valuable source of information about your audience's preferences and expectations. You can use analytics tools to monitor conversations on social networks and understand the trends and issues that concern your target audience.

Once you've identified your audience's issues and expectations, you can use this information to create stories that meet their needs. For example, if your target audience is concerned about environmental issues, you can create a story that highlights your company's sustainable initiatives. If your target audience is concerned about health issues, you can create a story that shows how your product or service can improve their health.

To find the story that will resonate with your audience, it's important to understand the issues and expectations of your target audience. By using different research techniques, you can identify the trends and concerns of your audience, and create stories that meet their needs.

2. Brainstorming: unleash your creativity to generate ideas

Effective brainstorming techniques to stimulate the imagination

Brainstorming is a creativity technique often used to generate original, innovative ideas. Here are some effective techniques for stimulating the imagination during a brainstorming session:

1. **The brainstorming method**: This is the most classic and best-known method of brainstorming. It involves bringing team members together and inviting them to exchange ideas on a given theme. Everyone can suggest ideas, which are noted down on a board or flip chart as they come up. The aim is to encourage the association of ideas and creative bounce-back.

2. **The SCAMPER method**: This method consists of exploring all possible ways of modifying or improving a product or service by asking a series of questions. SCAMPER is an acronym that stands for Substitute, Combine, Adapt, Modify, Put to another use, Eliminate and Reverse. This technique allows you to explore all possible avenues and stimulate your creativity.

3. **The 6 hats method**: This method was developed by Edward de Bono to encourage creative group thinking. It involves successively putting oneself in the shoes of six different characters, represented by hats of different colors: the white hat for neutrality and objectivity, the red hat for emotions and feelings, the black hat for criticism and analysis, the yellow hat for positivity and optimism, the green hat for

creativity and innovation, and the blue hat for synthesis and planning.

4. **The mind map method**: This method involves organizing your ideas in the form of a diagram, starting with a central keyword. The ideas are then linked together using branches, colors and images. This method visualizes the connections between ideas and stimulates creativity.

5. **Role-playing**: This method involves putting yourself in the shoes of a character or user to imagine scenarios and situations. Props, costumes and decorations can also be used to stimulate the imagination. This method allows you to project yourself into concrete situations and come up with original solutions.

By using these brainstorming techniques, you can unleash your creativity and generate original, innovative ideas for your storytelling. Remember, the important thing is to encourage ideas to flourish, without trying to judge or filter them.

Tips for organizing and evaluating brainstormed ideas

Once you've generated a large number of ideas during a brainstorming session, it's important to organize and evaluate them to find the ones that best suit your story. Here are a few tips to help you do just that:

- **Group ideas into themes**: group ideas that have similarities and connections to create broader themes. This will help you better understand key concepts and find ideas that align with your message.

- **Eliminate unnecessary ideas**: review all ideas and eliminate those that are not relevant or feasible. This will help you focus on the ideas that have the greatest potential for success.

- **Prioritize the remaining ideas**: once you've eliminated the ideas that aren't relevant, you can start evaluating the remaining ideas according to their feasibility, relevance and potential for success. Determine which ones are most important to your story and prioritize them.

- **Refine selected ideas**: work on selected ideas in detail, adding specific elements to make them more concrete. Try to find concrete examples and details that will help bring your ideas to life.

- **Test ideas**: before finalizing your story, test your ideas with your target audience. This will allow you to see how they react, and get feedback that will help you improve your story.

By following these tips, you'll be able to efficiently organize the ideas from your brainstorming session and come up with the best ideas for your story.

3. Research and inspiration: drawing on existing resources

How to draw inspiration from successful stories and campaigns to fuel your creativity

To find inspiration and feed your creativity in your quest to find the perfect story, it can be very helpful to look at stories and campaigns that have succeeded in the past. Researching and analyzing these stories can help you understand what has and hasn't worked for other brands.

There are several ways to draw inspiration from successful campaigns for your own storytelling. First, you can study the stories of your own industry or of brands similar to yours. This will help you understand how your target audience responds to different types of storytelling and advertising campaigns.

Then you can look at the campaigns of brands renowned for their successful storytelling, such as Nike, Coca-Cola or Patagonia, to name but a few. You can study their campaigns to understand how they used storytelling to create an emotional connection with their target audience.

Another method is to look at advertising campaigns that have won awards for creativity and impact. Awards such as Cannes Lions or Effies can be a source of inspiration for successful stories.

Finally, it can be useful to look outside your industry for inspiration. Sometimes, the most innovative and creative ideas come from other industries. For example, an advertising campaign for a technology company can be inspired by a successful campaign for a cosmetics company.

By studying these stories and campaigns, you can understand how storytelling has been used to create an emotional connection with audiences, and how it has been adapted to different social media platforms. It will also give you an idea of the types of storytelling and advertising campaigns that can work for your business.

However, it's important not to copy or imitate these stories directly. You must always be authentic and find your own voice, using the lessons you learn from these stories to guide your own creativity.

5. Choosing and refining your story

Steps to refine and perfect your story before telling it

Having developed a compelling story, the next step is to perfect it before presenting it to your audience. The first thing to do is ask yourself critical questions about the story. Ask yourself if it's coherent, if it's engaging and if it's convincing. You also need to make sure that your story is aligned with your brand values and that it matches your company's personality.

Next, you should consider how you're going to present your story. Depending on your target audience and your communication objective, you need to determine which format works best. For example, a visual story may work best for social media, while a more complex story may be better suited to a live presentation or longer-form content.

Once you've chosen your format, you need to work on the details of the story. Make sure your story is well structured, with a captivating introduction, an interesting development and a strong conclusion. Use elements of suspense to keep your audience interested, and make sure your story has a satisfying resolution.

You need to consider your audience's potential reactions. Anticipate any questions, objections or concerns your audience might have, and prepare appropriate responses. It's also important to be ready to adjust your story based on your audience's reactions and the feedback you receive.

To refine and perfect your story, you need to make sure that it's coherent, engaging and compelling, that it's aligned with your brand values and matches your company's personality. You also need to choose the format that best suits your target audience and work on the details of the story, using elements of suspense and ensuring a satisfying resolution. Finally, you need to anticipate your audience's reactions and be ready to adjust your story accordingly.

Chapter 9:

The great storytelling masters: how to draw inspiration from their stories?

Great storytellers are people who are able to tell captivating and inspiring stories in different fields, whether literature, cinema, advertising, entrepreneurship or politics. Their talent for storytelling enables them to arouse emotions in their audiences and mobilize them around a cause, an idea or a product.

1. David Ogilvy - Ogilvy & Mather

Its history

David Ogilvy is one of the 20th century's greatest masters of marketing and storytelling. Born in England in 1911, he began his career as a cook in the British army. After working in a variety of businesses, including cast-iron stove sales and cookie manufacturing, he moved to New York in 1948 to launch his own advertising agency, Ogilvy & Mather.

Ogilvy quickly achieved success as an advertising and marketing expert, and became famous for his innovative and creative advertising campaigns for brands such as Rolls Royce, Shell, and Dove. He is also known for popularizing the use of market research in the development of advertising campaigns.

Beyond his work in advertising, Ogilvy was a prolific writer and published several books, including "Confessions of an Advertising Man" and "Ogilvy on Advertising", which are still considered classics of marketing and advertising today. He died in 1999, but his legacy and influence on the world of advertising and storytelling are still palpable.

His well-known campaigns and his contribution to storytelling

Ogilvy's best-known campaigns include the Dove "Real Beauty" campaign, the Rolls Royce "Atmosphere" campaign, the Schweppes "Schhh... You Know Who" campaign, the Hathaway "Man in the Hathaway Shirt" campaign, and the campaign for porcelain brand Lenox. In each of these campaigns, Ogilvy used effective storytelling techniques to capture the audience's attention.

Dove's "Real Beauty" campaign

Ogilvy highlighted the importance of natural beauty, featuring women of different shapes and sizes in their ads. The campaign was a resounding success, as it enabled women to identify with the models presented and feel valued, which generated strong support from the female public.

His Rolls Royce "Atmosphere" campaign

Ogilvy created a unique brand narrative by presenting Rolls Royce cars as works of art, highlighting their elegance and timeless beauty. The campaign positioned the brand as a symbol of prestige and luxury, creating a strong, positive image in consumers' minds.

His Schweppes campaign "Schhh... You Know Who"

The campaign was also a success thanks to the creation of an iconic advertising character. The "Schhh" character was designed to represent the brand's unique quality, creating a strong and memorable image for consumers.

His Hathaway "Man in the Hathaway Shirt" campaign

It was a success thanks to the creation of a mysterious, sophisticated advertising character. The campaign featured a man wearing a Hathaway shirt, presenting him as a symbol of refinement and sophistication. The campaign enabled the brand to position itself as upscale and sophisticated, creating a unique and effective storytelling.

In terms of contributions to the art of storytelling, David Ogilvy is renowned for his scientific and rigorous approach to advertising. He has applied market research techniques to better understand consumer needs and expectations, and used this understanding to create effective, targeted advertising campaigns. He also emphasized the importance of creativity and emotion in storytelling, creating ads that touched consumers on a personal and emotional level.

Ultimately, David Ogilvy is a master storyteller because of his ability to create memorable advertising campaigns.

2. Seth Godin - Yoyodyne Entertainment

Its history

Seth Godin is an American author, blogger and speaker who has made a name for himself in the world of marketing and business by coming up with innovative ideas and pushing the boundaries of creativity. Born in 1960 in Mount Vernon, New York, Godin studied computer science and philosophy at Tufts University before going on to the Stanford Graduate School of Business.

After working for a number of companies, including Spinnaker Software, Seth Godin founded Yoyodyne Entertainment in 1995. The company was one of the first to use permission marketing, a technique that involves obtaining consumers' consent before sending them personalized advertising. Yoyodyne Entertainment has helped numerous companies develop innovative and effective marketing campaigns.

In 1999, Yoyodyne Entertainment was sold to Yahoo! and Seth Godin worked for the company for a time. He then left Yahoo! to devote himself to writing books and lecturing on marketing and entrepreneurship.

Seth Godin is the author of several New York Times bestsellers, including "Permission Marketing", "Purple Cow", "The Dip" and "Tribes". In these books, he encourages entrepreneurs and marketers to think outside the box and adopt innovative, creative marketing strategies. His books have influenced many marketing and business professionals, and have been translated into several languages.

Seth Godin is also a popular speaker who has delivered inspirational speeches at numerous conferences and events. His presentations are known for being energetic and motivating, and he often uses real-life examples to illustrate his ideas.

Beyond his professional success, Seth Godin is also known for his philanthropic commitment. He founded The Domino Project, an initiative to help authors publish their books independently, as well as the Acumen Fund, a non-profit organization dedicated to solving the problems of global poverty.

His story is that of an innovator who succeeded in rethinking marketing and encouraging professionals to adopt bold, creative strategies. His career is a source of inspiration for all those seeking to change the business world and make a difference in their field.

His well-known campaigns and his contribution to storytelling

Godin made a significant contribution to popularizing the concept of "permission marketing". According to Godin, permission marketing involves obtaining consumers' consent to communicate with them, rather than bombarding them with unsolicited advertising. He argues that companies need to offer consumers incentives to obtain their permission, such as relevant content and exclusive offers.

Godin helped popularize the concept of tribes. According to him, tribes are groups of people who share common values and interests, and who can be brought together around a brand or an idea. He argues that companies need to create tribes to build customer loyalty and generate commitment.

As for Godin's well-known campaigns, one of his most famous is the campaign for the Asics Gel-Kayano running shoe. This campaign was created in collaboration with the Publicis agency and involved the creation of an interactive website that allowed users to personalize their own pair of Gel-Kayano shoes. The campaign won several awards, including a Golden Lion at Cannes.

Godin is also known for his campaign to launch the Nissan Coupé convertible. The campaign included a series of commercials featuring people "living life large" while driving a Nissan Coupé convertible. The campaign won an Effie Award for advertising effectiveness.

Seth Godin is a master storyteller who has popularized concepts such as permission marketing and tribes. He is known for his creative and effective campaigns, which have helped evolve the field of marketing. His contribution to the advertising and marketing industry will continue to be studied and used as a source of inspiration for future generations.

3. Leo Burnett - Leo Burnett Worldwide

Its history

Leo Burnett was born in Illinois, USA, in 1891. After studying journalism and advertising, he worked in various agencies before founding his own advertising agency, Leo Burnett Company, in 1935 in Chicago. Leo Burnett is known for his creativity and unique approach to marketing. He was convinced that ads had to tell a story and create an emotion in the viewer to be effective.

Throughout his career, Leo Burnett has created iconic advertising campaigns for brands such as

Kellogg's, Coca-Cola, McDonald's, Marlboro and Procter & Gamble. His philosophy was to "focus on people", meaning he sought to understand consumers' needs, desires and behaviors to create ads that touched and inspired them.

Leo Burnett passed away in 1971, but his agency continues to thrive and is today one of the world's leading advertising agencies. His philosophy and approach to storytelling continue to inspire marketers the world over.

His well-known campaigns and his contribution to storytelling

Leo Burnett's best-known campaigns include :

- **Marlboro**: Burnett transformed Marlboro from a cigarette brand for women into a cigarette brand for men, using the cowboy character as a symbol of virility. The "Marlboro Man" campaign was a huge success and became emblematic of American pop culture.

- **Tony the Tiger**: Burnett created the Tony the Tiger character to promote Frosted Flakes children's cereal. With his slogan "They're Great!", Tony became one of the most recognizable advertising characters of all time.

- **Jolly Green Giant**: Burnett also created the Jolly Green Giant character to promote canned vegetables. The smiling giant quickly became a familiar character to consumers and is still used in the brand's advertising.

Leo Burnett has made many contributions to the world of storytelling in advertising. He encouraged advertisers to focus on consumers' emotions and values rather than on the features of the products themselves. He was also a forerunner of creative advertising, encouraging his teams to think outside the box and find innovative ways of telling stories to sell products.

He has had a huge impact on the world of advertising and storytelling. His creative and emotional campaigns have inspired many generations of advertisers and helped shape the way we tell stories to sell products.

4. Bill Bernbach - DDB Worldwide

Its history

Bill Bernbach was an American advertising executive born in 1911. He began his career in a small advertising agency and eventually founded his own agency, Doyle Dane Bernbach (DDB), in 1949.

Bernbach is considered one of the pioneers of modern advertising, and has had a major influence on the advertising industry as we know it today. His creative approach to advertising helped shape the industry and raise the standard of advertising. Bernbach passed away in 1982, but his impact on the advertising industry is still felt today.

His well-known campaigns and his contribution to storytelling

Bill Bernbach is an American advertising executive and creative director who helped shape the modern advertising industry. He is best known for his contribution to the creation of the advertising agency Doyle Dane Bernbach (DDB), where he emphasized creativity and innovation, breaking with the practices of the time.

One of DDB's best-known advertising campaigns is undoubtedly that for Volkswagen, entitled "Think Small" in 1959. This campaign was developed in response to a request from Volkswagen to conquer the American market at a time when American cars were larger and more powerful. Bernbach chose to go against the grain of advertising at the time, using a minimalist format with simple illustrations, small pictures and catchy text. The campaign was a resounding success, helping Volkswagen conquer the American market.

Bernbach was also one of the first to use humor in advertising, as evidenced by his famous campaign for the Avis brand entitled "We Try Harder". This campaign was launched in 1962 to rival the Hertz brand as the market leader in car rental. Instead of claiming to be number one, DDB's campaign chose to highlight the extra efforts Avis makes to offer better service to its customers. The use of humor conveyed the message in a light-hearted and memorable way, and the campaign helped Avis double its sales in three years.

Finally, Bernbach also pioneered the use of customer testimonials in advertising, a technique now commonplace in modern advertising. One of DDB's most famous campaigns in this field was for the Champion sportswear brand, entitled "You Gotta Sweat". This campaign used testimonials from famous athletes to illustrate the benefits of Champion sportswear, with simple, hard-hitting messages such as "If you don't sweat, you don't win".

What Bill Bernbach brings to storytelling is, above all, a creative and innovative vision of advertising that breaks with the conventional practices of the time. His ability to take risks and use unprecedented techniques has enabled DDB to stand out from the crowd and create memorable, effective advertising campaigns. Bernbach also emphasized the importance of understanding human psychology in creating effective advertising, by understanding the needs and motivations of the target audience. Finally, Bernbach demonstrated the importance of using testimonials, humor and simple, straightforward messages to tell a compelling story.

5. The importance of these men for storytelling

These four men have left their mark on the history of advertising, each making a significant contribution to the world of storytelling.

David Ogilvy was one of the first to use consumer research and understanding to develop effective advertising campaigns. He also emphasized the use of storytelling to sell products, and popularized techniques such as using testimonials from satisfied customers to promote brands. His influence on the advertising world was considerable, and his methods continue to be studied and used today.

Seth Godin, meanwhile, brought an innovative vision to storytelling. He has emphasized the importance of emotional connection with audiences, and encouraged brands to tell stories that generate interest and engagement. His advertising campaigns often focus on ideas and concepts rather than specific products, which has changed the way brands communicate with their audiences.

Leo Burnett pioneered the use of fictional characters to promote products, creating characters such as Tony the Tiger for Kellogg's and the iconic lumberjack for Marlboro. He also encouraged the use of music and humor to tell stories that elicit an emotional response from the audience. His influence on the advertising industry is still evident today, and his creative approach continues to inspire many marketing and storytelling professionals.

Finally, Bill Bernbach revolutionized the advertising industry by emphasizing creativity and message quality over quantity. He encouraged the use of storytelling and humor to grab consumers' attention, and advocated a more authentic, human approach to advertising. His approach has influenced many advertisers and marketers over the decades, and continues to inspire many successful advertising campaigns.

These four great storytellers have made significant contributions to the history of marketing, influencing the way brands tell stories and communicate with their audiences. Their legacy continues today, and can serve as inspiration for marketing professionals seeking to master the art of storytelling.

Chapter 10:

Measuring the impact of your storytelling: performance indicators and return on investment

In this chapter, I discuss the importance of measuring the impact of your storytelling using key performance indicators (KPIs) and evaluating return on investment (ROI). I present tips for selecting relevant KPIs, analyzing and interpreting the data, and evaluating the ROI of your storytelling.

1. Understanding key performance indicators (KPIs) for storytelling

The different KPIs relevant to evaluating the effectiveness of your storytelling

When using storytelling in a marketing strategy, it's important to measure the effectiveness of this technique so that we can adjust and improve our approach. To this end, there are several key performance indicators (KPIs) to consider.

First of all, engagement rate is an important KPI to consider. It measures user interaction with your content, whether through comments, shares or likes. A high engagement rate indicates that your audience appreciates your story and is engaged with your message.

Secondly, the number of views is also an important KPI. It measures the reach of your story and the visibility of your content. However, it's important to take into account the quality of the views. For example, if your story is seen by a large number of people, but only for a few seconds, it won't have the same impact as a full view.

Conversion rate is another KPI to consider. It measures the number of users who performed a desired action after viewing your story, such as purchasing a product or signing up for a newsletter. This measures the effectiveness of your story as a conversion tool.

Time spent on content is also important. This measures how long users have spent watching or interacting with your story. A longer time spent indicates that your story is interesting and engaging.

Finally, sentiment analysis is an interesting KPI to consider. It measures users' emotional reactions to your story. For example, if your story evokes positive and emotional reactions, this can help strengthen the connection with your audience and improve your brand image.

It's important to measure the effectiveness of your storytelling using a combination of relevant KPIs. This allows you to understand how your audience interacts with your story and adjust your approach accordingly to improve your performance.

2. Analyze and interpret data to measure the impact of your story

How to interpret the results to adjust and improve your story

Once you've collected the data on the impact of your story, it's essential to interpret it correctly so that you can adjust and improve your storytelling strategy. Here are a few tips to help you understand and interpret the results:

- **Analyze trends**: start by looking at the general trends in your data over a given period of time. For example, if you've collected data on a three-month marketing campaign, look at trends over the three months rather than focusing on daily data. This will enable you to see overall

163

fluctuations and understand the behavioral patterns of your audience.

- **Identify strengths and weaknesses**: by reviewing your results, identify the strengths and weaknesses of your story. This might include the most successful campaigns, the most popular messages, the best-performing channels, the most engaged audiences, etc. By identifying strengths and weaknesses, you can adjust your storytelling strategy to maximize impact and minimize weaknesses.

- **Compare with objectives**: compare your results with the objectives you set for your storytelling strategy. If you met or exceeded your objectives, consider the factors that contributed to this success and how you can replicate them in the future. If you didn't achieve your objectives, consider the possible reasons why, and how you can adjust your storytelling strategy to achieve your goals.

- **Use comments and feedback**: don't rely solely on numbers to assess the impact of your story. Comments and feedback from your audience are also invaluable in understanding how they feel about your story. Use this feedback to adjust your storytelling strategy and improve your story.

- **Be ready to adjust**: finally, be ready to adjust your storytelling strategy based on results and feedback. It's important not to get stuck in a strategy that isn't working or that can be improved. Be flexible and ready to make changes to maximize the impact of your story.

Data analysis is essential for measuring the impact of your story. By correctly interpreting the results, you can adjust and improve your storytelling strategy to maximize impact and achieve your objectives.

3. Evaluate the return on investment (ROI) of your storytelling

Methods for quantifying the benefits of your storytelling in financial and other terms

To assess the return on investment (ROI) of your storytelling, you need to quantify the benefits generated by your story in financial or other terms. Here are a few ways of doing this:

1. **Sales tracking**: If your story has helped to increase your sales, you can easily quantify the return on investment by comparing sales before and after your story was implemented.

2. **Website traffic analysis**: If your story has engaged your audience and generated traffic to your website, you can use web analytics tools to quantify the return on your investment. For example, you can evaluate the number of unique visitors to your website, the time spent on the site, the bounce rate and so on.

3. **Customer satisfaction surveys**: If your story has had a positive impact on your company's image and your customers' satisfaction, you can use satisfaction surveys to quantify the return on your investment. For example, you can evaluate the overall satisfaction rate, the recommendation rate, etc.

4. **Social media analysis**: If your story has been shared and generated engagement on social networks, you can use social media analysis tools to quantify the return on investment. For example, you can evaluate

the number of shares, comments, mentions, etc., that your story has generated.

Return on investment can be quantified in a number of ways, depending on the objectives of your story and your company.

So it's important to define your objectives from the outset, and choose the most relevant KPIs and evaluation methods to measure the effectiveness of your story.

How to determine whether your story has generated a positive return on investment

Consider the total cost of creating and implementing the story, including the time and resources invested. By comparing these costs with financial results or other measures of success, you can determine whether or not your story was profitable.

Note that ROI can be difficult to measure when it comes to storytelling, as it can be a long-term process and the results may be indirect or intangible.

For example, a successful storytelling campaign can improve brand awareness in the long term, even if it doesn't immediately generate sales.

So it's important to consider the long-term effects of your story on your brand and customer relationships.

Ultimately, ROI needs to be assessed against the specific objectives of your story and your business. It's important to define these objectives from the outset, and track the appropriate metrics to determine whether your story has been a success on all fronts.

Chapter 11:

Common storytelling mistakes and how to avoid them

In this chapter, I discuss the common mistakes people make when it comes to storytelling and tips on how to avoid them. I cover the pitfalls of lacking clarity, creating flat characters, using jargon or complex information, and ignoring the audience's needs. By sharing these tips, I hope to help you overcome these obstacles to create engaging and impactful stories.

1. Lack of clarity and consistency

The pitfalls of a poorly structured or incoherent story

A poorly structured or incoherent story can greatly reduce its impact and understanding with the audience. Here are some of the most common pitfalls to avoid:

1. **Lack of narrative structure**: without a clear narrative structure, your story is likely

to seem disorganized and difficult for the audience to follow. It's important to define the beginning, middle and end of your story, and to ensure that each part is clearly articulated.

2. **Too many details**: while details are important to bring your story to life, too many can overwhelm the audience and distract them from the essence of your story. So it's important to choose the details you want to include in your narrative wisely.

3. **Lack of coherence**: the story must be coherent and logical to be effective. If the elements of your story are contradictory or don't align with each other, it's likely to confuse people and reduce the impact of your message.

4. **Inappropriate tone**: the tone of your story must be adapted to your audience and the objective of your story. If it's inappropriate or ill-adapted, it risks missing its target.

5. **Problem of identification with the audience**: if your story doesn't take into account the expectations and aspirations of your target audience, it may not arouse their interest or their support.

6. **Lack of clarity**: the story must be clear and easy for the audience to understand. If it's too complicated, or if the ideas are not clearly expressed, it risks losing its audience.

In short, a poorly structured or incoherent story can derail your message, so it's important to avoid these pitfalls to maximize the impact of your storytelling.

2. Flat, implausible characters

Common mistakes in character creation

One of the most common mistakes made when creating characters for a story is to make them flat and implausible. This can happen when characters are stereotyped or lack depth. Characters need to be sufficiently developed for the audience to identify with them and feel an emotional connection to them. Flat characters can also undermine the story's credibility and make it difficult for the audience to become involved in the story.

Another common mistake when creating characters is to make them too perfect or too bad. Characters that are too perfect can seem unrealistic and uninteresting to the audience, while characters that are too bad can seem cartoonish and implausible. Characters need to be complex enough to be believable, but also interesting enough to make the audience want to know more about them.

Keep characters consistent throughout the story. Characters should not change personality or behavior abruptly or unexpectedly, unless justified by the story itself. Characters must remain consistent in personality and behavior throughout the story, so that the audience can follow their development and become involved in the story.

3. Some examples of storytelling campaigns that went wrong

Pepsi's 2017 ad campaign with Kendall Jenner

In 2017, Pepsi launched an advertising campaign with model and reality TV personality Kendall Jenner, which quickly sparked controversy. In the ad, Jenner leaves a photo shoot to join a street protest, where she hands a can of Pepsi to a police officer, supposedly symbolizing the easing of tensions between protesters and law enforcement.

However, the campaign was criticized for its superficiality and lack of understanding of the reality of the protests and the social issues they raised. Many felt that the advertising was insensitive and offensive, as it seemed to exploit the protest movements to sell a product. The campaign was also accused of downplaying the serious problems facing the protesters, and of giving a false and simplistic image of reality.

The controversy had a significant impact on the Pepsi brand, which quickly withdrew the advert and issued an apology. It showed the importance of understanding social issues and sensitivity to culture and communication trends when creating storytelling campaigns.

Dove's 2017 advertising campaign

Dove's 2017 advertising campaign was one of the most notable examples of storytelling gone wrong in recent years. In this campaign, Dove released an ad that featured a black woman removing her t-shirt to reveal a white woman. The ad caused immediate controversy online, with many critics claiming that the ad was racist and offensive. The campaign was quickly withdrawn and Dove apologized, claiming that the ad was not intended to be racist but had been misinterpreted.

This campaign highlighted the importance of representation and diversity in storytelling. If you want to tell a story that resonates with your audience, it's crucial to understand their experiences and perspectives, especially when it comes to sensitive topics such as identity. It's also important to be cautious about using images or symbols that can be interpreted in a negative or offensive way.

The Dove campaign was an example of the need to think through all the possible implications of a story before publishing it. It's important to consider all angles and test with different audiences to make sure the story is clear, consistent and relevant to your audience.

McDonald's 2018 advertising campaign

The ad adopts a cinematic style, telling the story of a young boy who asks his mother about his deceased father. In the course of the conversation, the duo visit a McDonald's where they order a fish-and-batter sandwich, presented as his father's favorite dish. This revelation brings the boy closer to his father and comforts him.

The advertisement provoked a strong reaction from children's aid associations, who denounced the exploitation of a parent's death to sell hamburgers. The campaign was widely criticized on social networks, forcing McDonald's to withdraw the ad from all media.

This controversy highlights the importance of sensitivity and delicacy in storytelling. Brands need to take into account the values and emotions of their target audience and avoid potentially sensitive or controversial subjects.

An art to be mastered

Storytelling can be a powerful tool for achieving your communication objectives, but it can also be a pitfall if you don't watch out for some common mistakes.

Clarity and coherence are essential to make your story understandable and memorable. Flat, implausible characters can also ruin the effectiveness of your story. Finally, examples such as the ill-fated advertising campaigns of Pepsi, Dove and McDonald's demonstrate the importance of thinking carefully about the implications and possible interpretations of your story.

It's crucial to consider your audience and brand values to avoid missteps and create a compelling, relevant story.

Storytelling is a complex art that requires careful thought, but the rewards can be considerable if you practice it carefully.

Give your honest opinion on Amazon!

Your suggestions and criticisms are invaluable.

They make every reading experience even more satisfying!

Thank you very much for reading my book.

I wish you all the success you deserve!

Conclusion

As we come to the end of our journey through "The Art of Storytelling", I hope you've been able to grasp all the magic and power of stories, and their crucial role in marketing and communication. Stories have a unique ability to touch our hearts, unite us and bring our experiences and ideas to life.

During our journey together, we explored the foundations of storytelling, learned to recognize the key elements that make a story captivating, and discovered the secrets to creating emotional and inspiring narratives. We also explored how storytelling can be used to add soul to your business and strengthen the connection with your audience.

Now it's time to put everything you've learned into practice. Remember that the art of storytelling is a constantly evolving process, and your journey as a storyteller is just beginning. Keep experimenting, learning and honing your skills to create ever more powerful and memorable stories.

Beyond techniques and strategies, remember that storytelling is above all about passion and authenticity. Don't hesitate to share your experiences, your emotions and your vision of the world with your audience. It's by being sincere and touching the hearts of your readers that you'll succeed in creating stories that stand the test of time and leave a lasting impression.

Finally, remember that storytelling is an art to be shared and passed on. Don't hesitate to talk to other storytellers, draw inspiration from their tales and share your own. Together, we can perpetuate the age-old art of storytelling and continue to shape our world through the stories we tell.

I wish you every success and pleasure in your journey as a storyteller. May your stories be captivating, moving and inspiring, and may you always find magic and beauty in the art of storytelling.

Good luck, and may the adventure continue!

Thomas Deville

Printed in Great Britain
by Amazon